People and Life 4

People and Life 4

Author Jack McBain
Publisher Chung Kyudo
Editors Kwak Bitna, Cho Sangik
Designers Park Bohee, Yoon Hyunju

First Published March 2018
By Darakwon Inc.
Darakwon Bldg., 211, Munbal-ro, Paju-si, Gyeonggi-do 10881
Republic of Korea

Tel. 82-2-736-2031 (Ext. 553)

Price ₩14,000
ISBN 978-89-277-0936-7 14740
978-89-277-0932-9 14740 (set)

http://www.darakwon.co.kr

Main Book / Free MP3 Available Online
7 6 5 4 3 2 1 18 19 20 21 22

People and Life 4

Introduction

People and Life 4 is the last book in a four-level series for adult and young adult learners of English. This dynamic series contains material appropriate for students ranging from a beginning level to an intermediate level. Each book in the series provides more challenging material in order to meet the linguistic needs of a diverse community of language learners.

People and Life 4 has 12 units, each of which consists of a warm-up, 4 supporting lessons, and a wrap-up, which serves as a review of the unit. The book covers a variety of topics set in a Western sociocultural context. Students will find topics such as A.I., personal finance, and emergencies interesting and relevant. Topics that are accessible and relevant to a student's life make learning English easier and more fun.

As a multi-skill course book, *People and Life 4* introduces essential everyday English with speaking, listening, writing, reading, grammar, and vocabulary sections. However, the speaking and listening sections have been emphasized due to the critical importance of these two language skills. *People and Life 4* offers numerous opportunities for students to engage in conversations and participate in activities in English. Through these interactive, confidence-gaining, and interesting activities, students can develop their communication skills and make progress toward greater competence in English.

Author's Acknowledgments

The author would like to express his most sincere gratitude to the editor Bitna Kwak. Without her tireless work and guidance, this project would not have been possible. He would also like to acknowledge the contributions of Mr. Michael Putlack and the entire Darakwon management and staff. Finally, he would like to extend a heartfelt thanks to his family, who have been incredibly patient during the writing process of this book.

Scope and Sequence

Unit	Learning Outcomes	Speaking
Unit 1 Hopes and Dreams p.11 India was incredible! I'm dropping out. The Learning Annex The Appalachian Trail	*Students can . . .* talk about traveling vs. finding a job talk about their dream jobs discuss learning new skills later in life talk about the things they would like to achieve	Work and travel Describing a dream job Outlining a course
Unit 2 A.I. p.21 Siri, where is the Taj Mahal located? Do you want to live forever? Have you seen the movie *A.I.*? A Movie Review	*Students can . . .* talk about the positives and negatives of A.I. talk about modern and future technology discuss science-fiction films that deal with the topic of A.I. create the story for a science-fiction film	A.I.: positives and negatives Modern technology Future technology A science-fiction film An original science-fiction film idea
Unit 3 Different Perspectives p.31 It's cold in here. My boss is crazy! This room is too dirty. The 5 Love Languages	*Students can . . .* talk about resolving differences talk about areas of a relationship or partnership discuss problems with people at work talk about differences with travel partners describe the qualities of a good romantic partner	Types of accommodations Describing friends or partners Planning a trip Your love language
Unit 4 Mysteries p.41 He believes in Bigfoot. Have you ever seen a UFO? Is there life on other planets? The Pyramids and Orion's Belt	*Students can . . .* talk about the paranormal talk about mysterious things they have seen describe some of Earth's ancient mysteries talk about intelligent life on other planets	Presenting a paranormal topic A strange sighting Researching an unsolved mystery Life on other planets
Unit 5 Priorities p.51 She thinks I work too much. Here's what you should do. I need a little more "me" time. It's as simple as ABC!	*Students can . . .* talk about their priorities in life talk about prioritizing tasks talk about productive activities vs. unproductive ones talk about their A, B, and C lists of priorities	A list of priorities A to-do list Productive vs. unproductive activities A perfect day Your ABC priorities
Unit 6 Genetics p.61 Am I losing my hair? Designer Babies Stem Cell Therapy Are you a super-sleeper?	*Students can . . .* talk about their genetic traits discuss medical breakthroughs and pregnancy talk about future medical breakthroughs talk about cloning	Traits you share with your family Interesting medical breakthroughs

Grammar	Listening	Vocabulary	Reading / Writing
Need + infinitive/gerund *I thought you had, I think you will* *Make* + noun	A job lead Dream jobs Learning new skills	Kinds of classes offered at a community center	**Reading** *The Appalachian Trail* **Writing** When to achieve one's dreams
	The singularity My parents, the technophobes The movie *Minority Report*	Modern and future technology Phrasal verbs with *Come*	**Reading** *A Movie Review* **Writing** Making a film
	The wedding guest list New managers Unhappy with a hotel room	Phrasal verbs with *Put* Types of accommodations	**Reading** *The 5 Love Languages* **Writing** The most romantic person
	Ghost hunters A UFO sighting Easter Island and Stonehenge	The paranormal Verbs of perception	**Reading** *The Pyramids and Orion's Belt* **Writing** A mysterious place you would like to visit
	A change in plans A to-do list My perfect day	Common reductions Useful verbs for planning a business trip	**Reading** *It's as Simple as ABC!*
	Mother's or father's traits Designer babies Organ transplantation	Words related to genetics Asking for clarification / repetition Getting someone's attention Inherited illnesses	**Reading** *Are You a Super-Sleeper?* **Writing** What are your genetic gifts

Grammar	Listening	Vocabulary	Reading / Writing
Hope vs. *wish*	Applying for a bank loan A brother's bad spending habits Financial advice from an expert	Purchasing a home Credit cards	**Reading** *Dear Mom and Dad* **Writing** A letter asking to borrow some money
Infinitives as object complements	A dangerous problem with a defective phone A stroke or heart attack Instructions for a fire drill and an extreme weather drill	Kinds of emergencies	**Reading** *Survivor's Guilt* **Writing** Surviving a tragedy
Time adverbials	The mammoth The passenger pigeon Diseases and vaccinations	Extinction and the environment	**Reading** *How Did the Dinosaurs Go Extinct?* **Writing** An endangered animal
Past modals	A Korean mountain climber Bernadette's three pieces of advice Risks that did and did not pay off	Starting a company	**Reading** *Michaela's Jujitsu School* **Writing** Describing a dream in three steps
	Is Pluto a planet? Spacewalking A Mars colony	NASA inventions Phrasal verbs with *Work*	**Reading** *Going Up?* **Writing** Would you travel to Mars?
Causative verbs	A graduation party Dream jobs After graduation	Celebrations / special events	**Reading** *The Wedding Planner* **Writing** Describe your perfect wedding

Getting Ready

Let's learn some useful classroom expressions.

Your teacher says . . .

Find a partner.
Get into groups of three/four/etc.
Stand up and mingle. Then ask your classmates the questions.
Share your opinions/ideas.
Present your ideas to the group/class.

Students give advice and share opinions . . .

I think . . .
I think you / we should . . .
In my opinion, we should . . .
If I were you, I would . . .
Why don't you / we . . . ?
I totally agree with you.
I strongly disagree.

Unit 1 Hopes and Dreams

Warm-up

A Look at the pictures. What are their dreams?

B What dreams have you achieved in your life? What do you hope to achieve?

India was incredible!

Conversation

Listen and practice the conversation. 01-01

A How was your trip to India, Allen?
B India was incredible.
A Where did you go?
B I went all over. Here's a picture of me at Bhagsunag Falls.
A It's beautiful. How long were you in India?
B Just over four months.
A Four months? How did you get that much time off from work?
B I didn't. I quit my job. I gave my boss two weeks' notice and left the day after my last day of work.
A Wow! I'm too scared to do what you did.

Group Work

A Make a group of five students. Then write your answers to the two survey questions in the table. After that, complete the table by asking your group members the two questions.

Student's Name	Which is more important: traveling or making money?	Why do you think one is more important than the other?
Me		

B Summarize the survey results by using the prompts in the speech balloon. Then choose a group representative to present the results to the class.

More than half of the students in this survey believe traveling is (more / less) important than making money. ________ students said they think ________________________________. On the other hand, ______ students thought ______________ is important because ___________________________.

Listening

A Listen to the conversation and answer the questions. 01-02

1. Where does the woman live?
   a. Hollywood Hills
   b. Los Feliz
   c. Culver City
2. What kind of studio is the woman an intern for?
   a. a studio that produces cartoons
   b. a studio that produces action movies
   c. a studio that does live performances
3. How does the woman earn money?
   a. She does housework.
   b. She draws cartoon characters.
   c. She serves drinks.
4. How much longer will the woman's parents give her money?
   a. eight months
   b. one year
   c. four months
5. How does the man help the woman?
   a. He lends her some money for the rent.
   b. He promises to give her a good job lead.
   c. He introduces her to someone famous.

B Listen again and choose True or False.

1. It was cold in Los Angeles when Millie called Chang. [True / False]
2. Internships are usually paid. [True / False]
3. Millie works in a restaurant. [True / False]
4. Millie's dream is to work in the entertainment industry. [True / False]
5. The man's uncle has offered Millie a job. [True / False]

Pair Work

Imagine you are going abroad for an extended period of time. Then write the information about your journey in the table and share it with your partner.

Travel Period e.g. From August 1st to September 10th		
Number of Countries You can plan to travel to more than two countries.		
Where are you going to visit?		
Flight	Seat	□ first class □ business □ economy
	Expected Fare	$________
Type of Accommodations	□ 5-star hotel □ guest house □ resort □ motel □ inn	
Items Needed e.g. cell phone, backpack, emergency medicine		

I'm dropping out.

Conversation

Listen and practice the conversation. 01-03

A Dad, I need to talk to you.
B What is it, Annie?
A I'm dropping out of school.
B But you've only got three more semesters left.
A I know, but I need to pursue my dream.
B Dancing? I thought you'd let that dream go by now.
A I haven't. I can't stop thinking about it. I want to be a professional dancer.
B It's a difficult life. You won't make a lot of money, at least not in the beginning of your career. And dancers get injured, too.
A I know, but my dream is to become a Broadway dancer, and I'll never forgive myself if I don't at least try.
B If that's how you feel, then your mother and I will support your decision.

Useful Expressions

A Let's learn some useful expressions.

need + infinitive **need + gerund (passive voice)**	You **need to wash** your car. Pam **needs to see** a doctor. The closet **needs organizing**. The windows **need washing**.
I thought you had + past participle The speaker thought the event had already finished.	Billy **thought** she **had forgotten** about his birthday. We **thought** you **had** already **eaten** lunch.
I think you will + infinitive (without *to*) The speaker is making a prediction about a future event.	They **think** you **will enjoy** your time abroad. Chris and Zack **think** you **will do** well on the next exam.
make + noun	Mike knows the restaurants in this city well, so he should **make a suggestion**. Joey will **make a** good **decision**. Junhee should **make an effort** to get an A in math.

B Fill in the blanks with the correct words or expressions.

1. Dad, I really ________ to talk to you. It's urgent!
2. Hannah said she would ________ a phone call when she arrives home.
3. I ________ Sarah ________ do great tonight in the performance. She has practiced a lot.
4. They ________ plans to go to India during summer vacation.
5. Your car is really dirty. It ________ washing.
6. Melissa ________ her boyfriend ________ forgotten about Valentine's Day, but then he gave her a gold necklace at the end of the night.

Listening

A Listen to the talks and change the false statements into true statements. 01-04

1-2

1. Kayla wanted clothes as birthday and Christmas presents when she was young.
2. Kayla is moving to Paris in three months.

3-4

3. Justin travels around the world rapping.
4. Justin plans to study business when he is too old to perform with X Street.

B Complete the information cards according to each person's story.

Kayla

Age:
Dream Job:
Current Status:

Justin

Age:
Dream Job:
Current Status:

Group Work

A Complete the information about your dream job.

My Dream Job

Job Title

Description

Salary

Hours

Skills Necessary

More Information
e.g. pros and cons, related company names, working environment

B Now share the information about your dream job with your group members.

The Learning Annex

Conversation

Listen and practice the conversation. 01-05

A You look depressed, Walter. What's wrong?

B I'm forty years old, I'm divorced, and I hate my job.

A Come on. Cheer up. You have a great job, you're funny, and forty is still young.

B I need a change. I'm thinking about quitting my job and becoming a writer.

A Really? That sounds like a terrible idea to me.

B Why?

A Because you make good money at your job. And if you quit, you'll be broke.

B I have some savings.

A And when your savings are gone, what will you do then?

B I'll figure something out.

A Listen. Why don't you attend a writing class at the Learning Annex to see if you really enjoy writing? That way, you can make a living and follow your dream.

B That's a pretty good suggestion. How do I sign up?

Vocabulary

Match the words to the correct pictures.

1. ☐ Pilates
2. ☐ table tennis
3. ☐ car maintenance
4. ☐ calligraphy
5. ☐ handicraft
6. ☐ web design
7. ☐ drone flight
8. ☐ interior decorating

a.

b.

c.

d.

e.

f.

g.

h.

Listening

A Listen to the conversation and answer the questions. 01-06

1. Why is the woman learning Chinese?
   a. to learn about Chinese culture
   b. to talk more openly with her husband
   c. to communicate better with her in-laws

2. Why is learning Chinese easier for native English speakers?
   a. The languages sound similar.
   b. The languages have similar alphabets.
   c. The languages share similar grammatical structures.

3. What has the man just finished learning about at the community center?
   a. automobile repair
   b. Chinese
   c. computer science

4. What kind of car maintenance has the man done since taking the class?
   a. The man has brought his wife's car to a mechanic for an oil change.
   b. He has fixed a broken part on his car.
   c. He has performed a routine oil change.

5. What can be inferred about the man's wife?
   a. She's happy that her husband has found a new hobby.
   b. She's glad her husband can save the family some money.
   c. She's excited to have dinner with another couple.

B Listen again and choose True or False.

1. Stephanie is teaching a class at the community center. [True / False]
2. The man's wife has just completed a vehicle maintenance class. [True / False]
3. The woman thinks Chinese pronunciation is not that difficult. [True / False]
4. Stephanie plans to take a car maintenance class when her Chinese class is finished. [True / False]
5. The two couples went to a Chinese restaurant together. [True / False]

Making a Course Outline

Imagine you are running a course at a community center in your city and complete a course outline.

(year) Course Outline	Subject: ______________
Instructor	*Name:* *Department:* *Phone Number:* *Email Address:*
Class Time / Date e.g. half an hour / three times a week	
Course Summary	*In this class, students will...*
Course Objectives / Goals	*After taking this course, students can...*

The Appalachian Trail

Reading

A Read the letter. 01-07

Dear Mom and Dad,

I hope you guys are doing well. I've just finished my last exam of the semester, and I am excited for the summer. At Christmas, as you remember, I was talking about backpacking across Europe with my roommate, Simone. But that requires getting a passport and lots of money for airline tickets, hostels, and food. Then Simone told me about a really exciting backpacking opportunity right here in the United States: The Appalachian Trail. Before you get too worried or try to talk me out of it, let me tell you a bit about the history of the Appalachian Trail.

The idea for the A.T. began with a forester named Benton MacKaye. He came up with the idea shortly after his wife passed away in 1921. The trail reaches all the way from Georgia to Maine and goes along the Appalachian mountain range. That's why they call it the Appalachian Trail. I'm not going to be able to come home this summer because hiking the trail is going to take us all summer, and we won't even be able to finish half of it, as the trail is 3,500 kilometers in length. We're going to start here in Georgia, and then we'll stop somewhere in Pennsylvania. Simone's parents live there, so we'll stay at her house for a few days before we return to school in the fall.

Don't worry about money. I've saved up $2,000 from my part-time job, but it's not going to be that expensive to hike the trail. It isn't good to carry a lot of weight in your pack. Because of the long distance and hot weather, the less you have to carry, the better. Wish me luck, and by the way, I'll have my phone with me so I'll text you or send you emails from time to time so you will know we're safe. I'll send you an email with Simone's parents' information in it, too, so you can connect with them.

Love,

Mandy

Comprehension Check Answer the questions about the letter.

1. What kind of trip was Mandy planning during Christmas?
2. Why is it expensive to backpack across Europe?
3. Who conceived of the idea for the Appalachian Trail?
4. Where are Mandy and Simone going to start their hike? Where are they going to finish?
5. Why should hikers pack light for the Appalachian Trail?

B Do you think you would enjoy hiking the Appalachian Trail?

Survey

A Raise your hand if the item the teacher reads aloud is something you want to achieve in the future.

	How many		How many
• Travel overseas alone		• Donate a lot of money to the poor	
• Get fit		• Raise a pet	
• Get married and have a family		• Get a job with a high salary	
• Buy a house or an apartment		• Live in the city	
• Buy a fancy car		• Live in the country	
• Learn a musical instrument		• Live near the ocean	
• Write a novel		• Buy an expensive item	
• Record a song		• Become famous	

B Which item resulted in the most students raising their hands? And which item resulted in the least number of students raising their hands?

Wrap-up

A Fill in the blanks with the correct expressions: *need, make, ~ think ~ will,* and *~ thought ~ had.*

1. Mom didn't make any dinner for you. She __________ you __________ eaten.
2. April __________ an appointment to see Dr. Spencer for a regular dental checkup.
3. Allen __________ the kids __________ get along well, but I'm not so sure.
4. We __________ to call your mother.
5. Let's hope Jim will __________ a good deal with D&T Inc.
6. These dishes really __________ cleaning.
7. He __________ she __________ left the party without him.

B Think about a dream you would like to achieve in the future and answer the questions. Then tell your partner about your dream.

My Dream

What is your dream?

What are some challenges that might prevent you from achieving your dream?

How do you plan on overcoming these challenges?

What do you need to achieve your dream?

Who will help you achieve your dream?

My dream is to become an actor. I want to be the lead actor on a popular television drama. Many other people share the same dream as me, so I will have to compete with lots of other actors. I will study acting really hard. I will need to earn money to pay for acting classes. Maybe my parents will lend me some money, so I can pay for the expensive classes.

C Write a short paragraph about why you think it is or is not important to achieve your dreams before you start a family.

Unit
2
A.I.

Warm-up

Match the comments with the correct pictures.

a. I could receive treatment from a doctor who lives halfway around the world.
b. I wouldn't have to wait more than an hour to get things I ordered online.
c. I'd be able to chat with my friends without carrying around a heavy smartphone.
d. We'd get to work in no time because we'd fly over heavy traffic.
e. I could control the temperature, the lighting, and the music in my house from one device.
f. I could put my seat back and take a nap on my way to work.

1. ☐

2. ☐

3. ☐

4. ☐

5. ☐

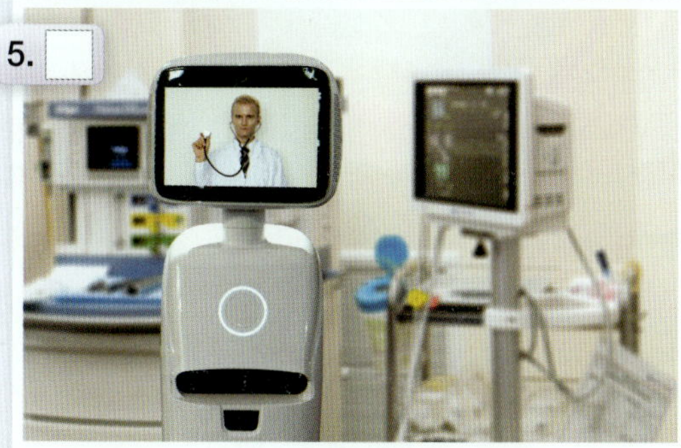

6. ☐

Siri, where is the Taj Mahal located?

Conversation

Listen and practice the conversation. 02-01

A Where is the Taj Mahal, Xiang?
B It's in India.
A I know it's in India, but what city is it in?
B It starts with an "A."
A That's right, "A" something.
B Argo... Arga?
A No, that's not it. Just a sec. Siri, in which city is the Taj Mahal located?
S The Taj Mahal is located in the city of Agra.
A That's right. Agra! Thanks, Siri!
B That's so funny.
A What's so funny?
B You just thanked a computer.
A I guess you're right. The voice just makes her sound so human.
B Now ask her why you don't have a girlfriend.
A Very funny.

Vocabulary

A Match the words with the correct definitions.

cyborg robotics artificial intelligence autonomous car
virtual reality technophobe technophile computer literate

1. ____________ someone who doesn't like new technology and is afraid to use it
2. ____________ an environment which is produced by a computer and seems like reality to the person experiencing it
3. ____________ someone who is enthusiastic about technology
4. ____________ a being that is part human and part machine; a machine that looks like a human being
5. ____________ the science of designing and building robots
6. ____________ a type of computer technology which makes machines work in an intelligent way similar to the way that the human mind works
7. ____________ a vehicle that is capable of sensing its environment and navigating without human input
8. ____________ knowledgeable about computers; able to use a computer

B Do you know anyone who is a technophile or a technophobe? If yes, tell your partner about him or her.

Listening

A **Listen to the talk and change the false statements into true statements.** 02-02

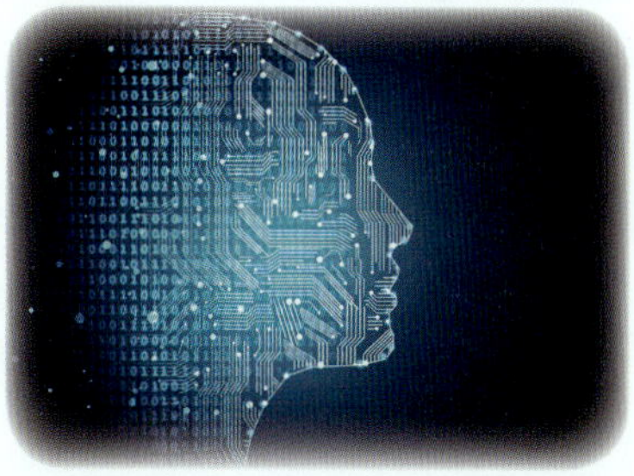

1. The term "singularity" was coined in 1905.
2. The singularity is the idea that human intelligence will one day surpass artificial intelligence.
3. Most experts agree the singularity will occur at the end of the century.
4. Some scientists imagine a peaceful future where machines enjoy more leisure time.

B **Listen again and write the correct words in the blanks.**

1. The phrase "the singularity" was created by ______________ John von Neumann.
2. It's possible that A.I. will no longer need human programmers to ______________ its performance.
3. Some scientists predict a future where robots have ______________ beyond any need for humans.
4. Other scientists imagine a future where humans ______________ side by side with machines.

Group Work

A **Write two lists of the positives and negatives associated with artificial intelligence. If necessary, you can use the Internet.**

Positives of A.I.	Negatives of A.I.
ex. *We will get more leisure time.*	ex. *Humans will become irrelevant.*
(1)	(4)
(2)	(5)
(3)	(6)

B **Give a group presentation about your lists by using the prompts below.**

I'd like to talk about the positives and negatives of A.I. First, the benefits of A.I. are (1), (2), and (3). The downsides are (4), (5), and (6).

Do you want to live forever?

Conversation

Listen and practice the conversation. 02-03

A I came across a really interesting video on OnTube this morning.
B What was it about?
A It was about computers and immortality. They say computers might allow us to live forever.
B How is that possible?
A The scientist in the video believes that we will someday be able to upload our consciousness onto a computer hard drive.
B What do you mean by consciousness?
A Our memories—everything we've learned and experienced during our lifetimes.
B Okay, I see. But how will that allow us to live forever?
A Once we are able to upload all of the information from our brains onto a computer hard drive, we won't need bodies any more. We will exist within a computer network.
B That's really interesting and really scary.
A I know.

Useful Expressions

A Let's learn about phrasal verbs using *come*.

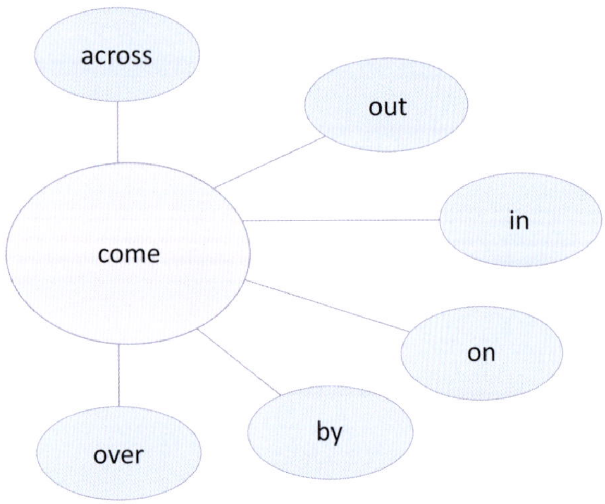

Examples
Diane **came across** an old yearbook in a box in her parents' attic.
Come out with us on Friday night.
Can I **come in**?
Oh, **come on**! They lost again? This soccer team stinks!
Why don't you and Darlene **come by** the house at seven o'clock?
Jules and Jeremy can't **come over** on Saturday.

B Read the sentences and choose the correct answers.

1. Please come (in / out), Harriet. I just made a pot of coffee.
2. Are Becky and Hyemin coming (across / out) with us on Friday night?
3. My mother came (across / by) my old yearbook the other day. The pictures were hilarious.
4. Is Jeanie going to come (over / in) to my house for brunch tomorrow? I want to give her a birthday present.
5. Paul, you should come (in / by) with your family on the weekend. Our kids can play soccer in the backyard together.

Listening

A Listen to the conversation and choose the correct answers. 02-04

1. Marie's phone bill is just (under / over) three hundred dollars.
2. Marie's father worked in (electronics / construction).
3. Marie and her siblings tried to teach their parents how to use a computer (three / two) years ago.
4. Marie's parents have a (laptop / P.C.).
5. Marie is probably going to (call / write) her parents in the future.

B Listen again and choose True or False.

1. Marie is frustrated because her parents are technophobes. [True / False]
2. Marie lives a long distance from her parents. [True / False]
3. Marie's mother worked in a childcare center. [True / False]
4. Marie's parents use their computer once a week. [True / False]

Pair Work Complete the technology questionnaire by asking your partner the questions in it.

Technology Questionnaire

1. Do you think technology has changed in the past ten years?
□ yes □ no

2. If yes, what kind of technology have you seen?
____

3. Do you have to buy the newest gadgets as soon as they are available?
□ yes □ no

4. If yes, what kinds of new gadgets have you recently bought?
□ smartphone □ computer □ MP3 □ VR (virtual reality) □ tablet PC □ other (________)

5. If no, what is the reason for keeping the old gadgets?
□ a lack of money □ familiarity with the old one □ a need to observe the contract period
□ time consuming to learn about a new one □ other (________)

6. What kind of technology would you like to see that does not currently exist?
____

7. What are some examples of technology that have made the world a better place?
____

Have you seen the movie *A.I.*?

Conversation

Listen and practice the conversation. 02-05

A Pedro, have you seen the movie *A.I.*?

B When did it come out?

A It came out in 2001.

B I think I saw it when I was in elementary school, but I don't remember it very well. What's it about?

A It's about a robot child whose dream is to become human. It's loosely based on the Carlo Collodi novel *Pinocchio*.

B How is it similar to the novel?

A In the novel, the puppet child Pinocchio dreams of someday becoming a real boy. In the movie *A.I.*, they've updated it so that instead of being a puppet, the child is a robot.

B Now I remember. David, the robot child, goes on a long journey with his talking teddy bear to find the blue fairy that he believes can make him human.

A Exactly. What did you think about it?

B I liked it a lot, although I found the ending difficult to understand.

A Me, too.

Group Work

A Make a group of three students and look at the popular movie titles about artificial intelligence. Then choose one of the movies and write correct information about the movie.

2001: A Space Odyssey | A.I. | The Terminator | Ex Machina | Blade Runner | I, Robot

Movie Title

Year

Plot Summary

How You Feel about the Movie

B Choose a group representative and make a presentation about the movie. Then listen to the other groups' presentations and write about one of the presentations.

Movie Title

Year

Plot Summary

How You Feel about the Movie

C Write a short essay comparing your group's movie to another group's movie.

Listening

A Listen to the talk and answer the questions. 02-06

1. What part of the police department does John Anderton work for in *Minority Report*?
   a. Pre-cog
   b. Pre-policing
   c. Pre-crime

2. Why must John Anderton go on the run?
   a. He's guilty of committing murder.
   b. He's accused of kidnapping a child.
   c. He's accused of killing someone.

3. Who wrote the book *The Minority Report*?
   a. Steven Spielberg
   b. Philip K. Dick
   c. John Anderton

4. Which sentence is NOT true about the book or movie?
   a. John Anderton is married in the book.
   b. John Anderton had a son in the movie.
   c. John Anderton had a son in the book.

5. Why does John Anderton so strongly believe in the pre-crime unit in the movie?
   a. He wants to eliminate crime before he starts a family.
   b. He wants to prevent crimes like the one his family experienced.
   c. He believes the police department can help him find his son.

B Complete Caleb's speech by filling in the blanks.

The movie title I watched is ______________.
It was released in ______. The movie is based on the book ________________, which was published in ______.

Presentation | A Science Fiction Film

Give a presentation about your favorite science-fiction film.

My favorite science-fiction film is *Wall-E*. It takes place in space in the distant future. Jeff Garlin is in it. It's about a small dirty trash-compiling robot named Wall-E. Wall-E meets a slick new robot named Eva. He follows her to a spaceship where humans now live because the Earth has become too polluted to live on. This is a spoiler, so cover your ears if you don't want to know the ending. In the end, the humans return to the Earth in order to rebuild their society.

A Movie Review

Reading

A Read the movie review by the blogger. 02-07

www.bobby'sscififilmblog.com/2001aspaceodyssey/review

Bobby's Sci-fi Film Blog

Hey, guys! We're going back to the year 1968 to review Stanley Kubrick's masterpiece *2001: A Space Odyssey*. In this film, we are brought aboard the spacecraft *Discovery One* as it travels toward the planet Jupiter. Because the time required to reach Jupiter is so great, some of the astronauts on the ship are kept in a state of suspended animation, or constant sleep. Although there are pilots on the ship, it is mainly controlled by a heuristically programmed algorithmic computer, or HAL. HAL's artificial intelligence allows it to think, reason, and learn. HAL sees the crew members through its ominous red camera lens and speaks to them in a menacingly calm voice. When the astronauts make a decision that jeopardizes the mission, HAL disobeys their orders. For HAL, nothing can be allowed to disrupt the true mission. (I don't want to spoil the movie for those of you who haven't seen it, but there's a secret reason that they are going to Jupiter that only HAL knows about.) The astronauts eventually realize that there's a serious problem with HAL and decide to shut it down. When HAL discovers their plan, it begins killing them one by one. In the end, the last living crew member, Dr. Bowman, is able to reach HAL's processor core and deactivate it by cutting all of its circuits.
Apart from the amazing special effects, especially for its time, the film does a great job of raising ethical questions about artificial intelligence. HAL had the ability to think like a human being, but it lacked a moral compass. HAL operated on only logic and reason, not emotion. In the movie, HAL's voice was always calm and gentle, but its actions were cruel and terrifying. This is a great movie and it really makes you think, so I definitely recommend *2001: A Space Odyssey*. Stream it today! Bye!

Bobby

Thank you for visiting my blog!

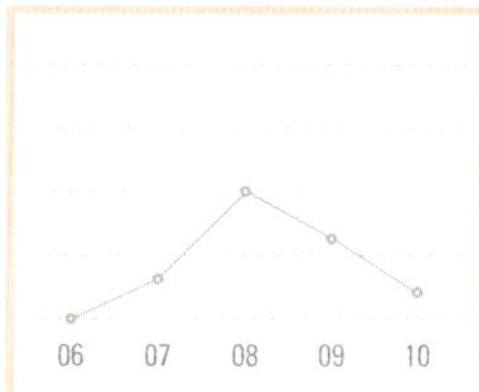

Comprehension Check **Answer the questions about the movie review.**

1. Why are some of the astronauts kept in a state of constant sleep?
2. How are the ship's operations controlled?
3. Why does HAL disobey the pilot's orders?
4. How does Dr. Bowman defeat HAL?
5. What was the problem with HAL's artificial intelligence?

B Have you seen this movie or read the Arthur C. Clarke book *2001: A Space Odyssey* was based on? If so, what did you think about it? If not, would you like to see the movie or read the book?

Group Work

A Look at the movie posters and choose one of them in order to create your own movie. Then write its title and a brief plot summary.

1.

2.

3.

Title ______________________

Plot Summary

B Make a group of five students and introduce the movie you created to your group members. Then complete the table by taking notes about your group members' movies and rating them.

Name	Movie Poster	Movie Title	Plot Summary	Your Rating
	1 / 2 / 3			☆☆☆☆☆
	1 / 2 / 3			☆☆☆☆☆
	1 / 2 / 3			☆☆☆☆☆
	1 / 2 / 3			☆☆☆☆☆

C Tell the class about the movie that you graded the highest.

I graded Mindy's movie the highest. She chose the first picture, and the title of her movie is *Earth Clone*. In the year 2200, Earth is so polluted that humans have to clone the planet in order to make a new, clean planet for people to live on. Unfortunately, the cloned Earth is smaller than the original one, so earthlings have to battle to find out who gets to live on the new planet.

Wrap-up

A Fill in the blanks with the correct prepositions: *across, by, in, on, out,* and *over*.

1. Lots of people walked by the shop, but not many came __________.
2. My mother came __________ some old pictures of us when we were young.
3. Sally said we should come __________ her house to pick up the table on Friday.
4. People are always coming __________ to your house. Isn't hosting guests all the time tiring?
5. Mr. Jacobs asked his workers to come __________ to dinner on Thursday evening.
6. Come __________! They missed another goal? This football team stinks!

B Imagine you owned an intelligent robot. Then talk with a classmate about what you would ask it to do in order to make your life easier.

There are several things I would ask my robot to do. First, I would ask my robot to clean my house and to cook all of my meals. Then, I would ask it to go the store to do all of my shopping. Finally, I would ask it to complete my tax forms. I hate doing my taxes!

C Choose three of the questions below and discuss them with your partner.

1. What is the most important technological innovation of the past 100 years?
2. Which electronic device that you currently own can you not live without?
3. Who is the most important technological innovator in your country?
4. Do you worry that A.I. will make our lives worse in the future?
5. What kinds of technological devices would you like to see in the future?
6. What current device would you like to buy but cannot afford right now?

D Choose one of the questions you and your partner discussed in C. Then write a short essay about your and your partner's answers to the question.

Different Perspectives

Warm-up

Look at the images. What do you see?

It's cold in here.

Conversation

Listen and practice the conversation. 03-01

A It's cold in here.
B I know.
A What's the temperature in here, like 17 or 18 degrees?
B Something like that.
A You're sitting right next to the thermostat. What does it say?
B Hmm. Let's see. Yup, it's 17 degrees in here. That's pretty cold.
A I wish I had the plaid blanket. Too bad it's in the bedroom.
B Yeah, me too. It's freezing in here.
A Achoo!
B Bless you.
A Fine! I'll get the blanket myself. It's like you don't even care about me!
B Huh? Are you angry?

Pair Work

Read about the situations in the table and ask your partner what he or she should do in each situation and why. Take turns asking and answering questions.

What should you do?		
1 You want to see the latest action movie, but your significant other wants to see the latest drama.	2 You want to have a quiet night at home for your anniversary, but your significant other wants to go out.	3 You want to live in an apartment in the city, but your spouse wants to live in a house in the suburbs.
4 You want to have children, but your spouse does not want to have children.	5 You want to take an evening class to learn Chinese, but your spouse wants to take an evening yoga class.	6 You want to visit your parents this weekend, but your significant other wants to go to the beach.

A What should you do if you want to see the latest action movie but your partner wants to see the latest drama?
B I would watch the latest drama with him and the latest action movie later by myself because I don't want to argue.

Listening

A **Listen to the two related conversations and answer the questions.** 03-02

1. Why was Cynthia upset with her fiancé?
   a. He dismissed an important conversation with her.
   b. He invited too many guests to their wedding.
   c. He refused to talk about the wedding with her.

2. What soccer teams were discussed in the talk?
   a. Barcelona and Manchester United
   b. Real Madrid and Barcelona
   c. Real Madrid and Chelsea

3. How did Cynthia act toward James after the game?
   a. She was terrified.
   b. She was warm.
   c. She was distant.

4. Who does James usually talk to after soccer matches?
   a. his brother
   b. his best friend
   c. his office friend

5. What can be inferred about James?
   a. He's fanatical about professional soccer.
   b. His work is more important than his home life.
   c. He doesn't really want to marry Cynthia.

B **Listen to the conversations again and choose True or False.**

1. James and Cynthia plan to get married in April. [True / False]
2. There will be a maximum of 50 guests at their wedding. [True / False]
3. Cynthia's friend thinks James was being self-centered. [True / False]
4. Real Madrid won the match 3–2. [True / False]
5. James finished talking to Frank at 9:30 p.m. [True / False]

Pair Work

Let's find out how strong you think you are in each of these areas of a relationship or friendship. Grade yourself from 1 to 5 with one being the worst score and five being the best score. Then talk to your partner about each category.

1. Communicating with your partner or friend	1	2	3	4	5
2. Listening to your partner or friend	1	2	3	4	5
3. Remembering special dates (anniversaries, birthdays, etc.)	1	2	3	4	5
4. Planning special occasions with your partner or friend (dates, parties, etc.)	1	2	3	4	5
5. Expressing love and emotions	1	2	3	4	5
6. Giving compliments	1	2	3	4	5
7. Staying connected	1	2	3	4	5
8. Laughing together	1	2	3	4	5

Total: ______ / 40

My boss is crazy!

Conversation

Listen and practice the conversation. 03-03

A I've got a problem, Alistair.

B What's that?

A My boss is crazy.

B How so?

A He tells me to do something one way, and then he changes his mind. It's maddening.

B Give me an example.

A Okay. Last week, he asked me to put copies of the daily schedules on everyone's desk first thing in the morning. So I started doing that.

B How was it done before?

A We used to email the schedules to everyone, but my boss thought people were ignoring the emails. That's why he wanted me to hand-deliver the copies.

B Okay, so what happened?

A This morning, while I was hand-delivering the schedules, he started yelling at me and accusing me of wasting time. He said I should just email them to everyone. He's so irrational.

Useful Expressions

A Let's learn about phrasal verbs using *put*.

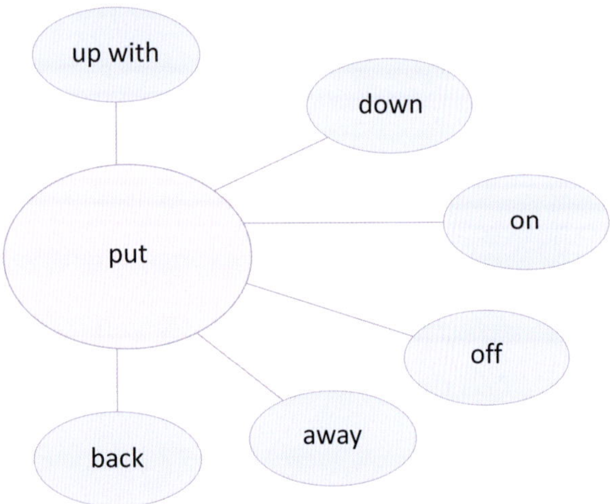

Examples
Suyoung couldn't **put up with** her boyfriend's mood swings any longer, so she broke up with him.
Put down your pencils, class. The exam is finished.
Jacob **put on** a suit and a tie for the dinner party.
Philip **put off** doing his assignment until the night before it was due.
The children always **put away/back** their toys. They are very thoughtful.
Justin decided to **put** the soda **back** and to buy water instead.

B Fill in the blanks with the correct prepositions.

1. Jane's boyfriend doesn't treat her very well. I don't think she should put ________ him any longer.
2. It is important to put ________ a hat before going outside. Too much sun can be dangerous.
3. The teacher scolded the children after playtime. She said, "If you take the blocks out, you have to put them ________ when you're done."
4. Abby should not put ________ studying for her exam. Organic chemistry is difficult, and she's going to need as much study time as possible.

Listening

A **Listen to the talk and answer the questions.** 03-04

1. Who is the speaker talking to?
   a. He is talking to company executives.
   b. He is talking to new managers.
   c. He is talking to the CEO.

2. What should managers never discuss with their staff?
   a. Managers should not talk about family.
   b. Managers should not discuss overtime.
   c. Managers should not discuss their pay.

3. Why do some new managers feel lonely?
   a. because they can no longer be friends with their former colleagues
   b. because they have too much work to do as new managers
   c. because they are often away on business and not in the office

4. What can change when someone is promoted to a management position?
   a. The person's former colleagues can feel bitter.
   b. The person's former colleagues will feel afraid.
   c. The person's former colleagues can become lazy.

5. What does the man say the best way to win over workers is?
   a. Be a generous manager.
   b. Be a competent manager.
   c. Be a fun and friendly manager.

B **Write the man's five-point plan.**

Five-Point Plan

1.
2.
3.
4.
5.

Writing

Discuss problems people usually have with others at work with your partner and answer the questions below. Then write a short essay using your answers.

- What problems do people usually have with others at work?
- Have you had any similar problems at school or work?
- Were you able to solve the problem? If yes, how did you solve it? If not, can you suggest a resolution to the problem?

This room is too dirty.

Conversation

Listen and practice the conversation. 03-05

A We're here. Isn't it great? It's right on the beach.

B This is where we're going to stay? There's no television or air conditioning.

A TV? We're on a tropical island in Thailand. We don't need TV.

B The room doesn't look very clean.

A It's only $9 per night. What do you expect? We'll spend most of our time exploring the island anyway.

B I don't want to stay here. There's a resort right up the street. Let's stay there.

A A resort costs between $50 and $100 per night.

B Yeah, but it will be clean and comfortable.

A I don't know. I thought we were going to backpack in Thailand. Staying in hotels and resorts is more like vacationing.

B This is a vacation for me. I took three weeks off from work to see Thailand and to have fun. I didn't pay to sleep in a room like this.

A Okay. Let's check out the resort. I hope it's not too expensive.

Vocabulary

Match the types of accommodations to the correct pictures.

a. 5-star hotel b. guest house c. resort d. bungalow e. motel f. inn

1. ☐

2. ☐

3. ☐

4. ☐

5. ☐

6. ☐

Listening

A Listen to the conversation and choose True or False. 03-06

1. The man is getting impatient waiting for the food. [True / False]
2. It is an overcast day in Miami. [True / False]
3. The woman is not very impressed with the hotel's amenities. [True / False]
4. The man remembered to bring the woman's sunscreen. [True / False]
5. The woman's opinion of the hotel changes. [True / False]

B Check the picture that matches the couple's current view from the hotel room.

1.

2.

3.

4.

Group Work

A With a budget of $1,000, plan a trip. Use whatever resources are necessary to find information for each category.

Plan a Trip

Destination & Length of Stay	______ for ____ days
Transportation	Price: $______
Accommodations	Price: $______
Food	Price: $______
	Total: $______

B Make a group of three or four students. Then have each group member give a brief presentation about his or her trip.

I am going to stay in a lakeside cabin two hours from the city for five days. I will drive, so the price of gasoline will be about $40. The cabin costs $50 a night, so it will cost $250 for the accommodations. I am going to stop at a grocery store on the way and buy food for the week. I plan on spending $400 on food and drinks. The total cost of the trip will be $690.

The 5 Love Languages

Reading

A Read the article. 03-07

Washington Daily Reader

LIFESTYLE

February 14th, 2018

Peggy O'Malley

Relationship Expert & Columnist

Happy Valentine's Day, readers! In this week's column, I want to talk to you about a book that has had a profound effect on my marriage. The book came out twenty-five years ago and was written by the author Gary Chapman. It is called *The Five Love Languages: How to Express Heartfelt Commitment to Your Mate*. The premise of the book is that there are five love languages and everyone has a specific preference for one of the primary "love languages." In order for us to feel truly loved by another, we must understand our partner's primary love language. The five love languages outlined in the book are gift giving, physical touching, words of affirmation, acts of service, and quality time.

The first year of marriage for my husband and me was very difficult. We argued all of the time, and we were terrible communicators. You see, my husband's primary love language is acts of service. But my primary love language is gift giving. Whenever my husband brought me flowers, my heart would sing. I felt so loved. But I also thought that he felt the same way when I gave him gifts. His reactions to my gifts were polite, but they did not elicit the enthusiastic reaction I had expected, and my feelings were often hurt. Had I cooked him his favorite meal or straightened up his office for him, he would have felt more loved.

It was not until I read Gary Chapman's book a short time later that I realized the error of my ways. I asked my husband to read it, too, and he found it equally insightful. We immediately started to see improvements in our relationship as we both became more attentive to each other's needs. Therefore, if you find yourself having difficulty communicating with your partner, perhaps you are not speaking the right love language. Run out and pick up a copy of *The Five Love Languages*. It might save your relationship.

Comprehension Check Answer the questions about the article.

1. How often does Peggy O'Malley write articles for the *Washington Daily Reader*?
2. When did the book *The Five Love Languages* come out?
3. What are Chapman's five love languages?
4. What is Peggy O'Malley's love language? How about her husbands?

B What is your love language?

My love language is words of affirmation. I really feel loved when my girlfriend gives me a compliment.

Group Work

A Make a group of four students and talk about something nice you have done for a romantic partner. Then complete the table by writing your group's answers in the table.

Name	What have you done for your romantic partner?
Me	

B Vote on who the most romantic person in the group is. Then write a short essay about him or her.

C Choose a group representative and let him or her make a presentation about your group's most romantic person.

Wrap-up

A Fill in the blanks with the correct prepositions: *up with, down, on, off, away,* and *back*.

1. Teachers cannot put __________ bad behavior in their classrooms.
2. My children are well behaved. They always put their toys __________.
3. Sally put __________ the heavy grocery bags as soon as she entered the apartment.
4. My brother is not a good student. He puts __________ his school assignments until the last minute.
5. Jay put the CD __________ on the shelf when he saw that the price was $45.
6. Janine put __________ her best dress for her date with Erik.

B Look at the pictures and describe each of the accommodations. Then say where you would like to stay if you were traveling or on vacation.

1.

2.

3.

4.

C Read about the situations in the table and say to your partner what you think you should do in each of the circumstances.

1

The parents of the person you've been dating for the past three weeks really want to meet you, but you feel uncomfortable meeting them so soon.

2

Your car runs well, but it's old and unattractive. You want to buy a new car, but your spouse wants you to drive the old one until it breaks down. That way you can save more money each month.

3

Your significant other likes to hold hands and hug in public, but you find these public displays of affection embarrassing.

4

You've been promoted to a managerial position at work, so now you're in charge of the people you used to work alongside. Whenever you're around, they behave differently and won't joke around with you.

D Talk about a problem you have had with someone recently. What happened, and how did it get resolved? Share your answer with your partner and then ask your partner how he or she would have resolved your problem.

Unit
4
Mysteries

Warm-up

A Discuss with your partner the meanings of the words in the picture. Use your dictionary if necessary.

B Look at the list of the world's greatest unsolved mysteries and share what you know about each of them with your partner.

The World's Greatest Mysteries

- Stonehenge
- UFOs
- aliens
- the pyramids
- the JFK assassination
- Bigfoot
- the Loch Ness Monster

He believes in Bigfoot.

Conversation

Listen and practice the conversation. 04-01

A I learned something really interesting about my coworker the other day.

B What's that?

A He believes in Bigfoot.

B What! That's crazy.

A I know. I thought he was joking. But he was dead serious.

B How does he defend believing in something like that?

A He thinks there are large, hairy, humanlike apes that live in northern Canada.

B Then why haven't we ever seen one before?

A He thinks they live so deep in the woods that we can't find them.

B Wow, that's so bizarre.

A Do you want to hear something even more bizarre?

B Sure.

A He's on vacation in northern Canada right now with a group of Bigfoot hunters. They're spending a week searching for evidence of Bigfoot.

B Wow, he's really dedicated.

Vocabulary | The Paranormal

Write the words in the correct places.

Bigfoot Martian poltergeist reincarnation fortunetelling Loch Ness Monster

1. 

2. 

3. 

4. 

5. 

6. 

Listening

A Listen to the conversation and answer the questions. 04-02

1. Why do the man and his wife like the show *Ghost Hunters*?
   a. They like it because they have personal experience with ghosts.
   b. They enjoy documentaries and scary movies, so the show appeals to them.
   c. They love fantasy programs, so they look forward to watching it each week.

2. What does "paranormal" mean?
   a. It means evident or obvious.
   b. It means strange but typical.
   c. It means odd or uncanny.

3. Why did the ghost hunters go to the Myrtles Plantation?
   a. People have seen ghosts there in the past.
   b. It is haunted by a famous ghost.
   c. It's the location of a famous horror movie.

4. What do you think the woman will probably do?
   a. She will cancel her weekly plans to watch the show.
   b. She won't start watching the show because of a time conflict.
   c. She will ask her boyfriend to stay home this weekend.

B Listen again and change the false statements into true statements.

1. The woman and her boyfriend always go out on Saturday nights.
2. The man and his wife enjoy horror movies and television dramas.
3. The ghost hunters recorded a video of a ghost.
4. The Myrtles Plantation is one of the most haunted locations in Louisiana.

Presentation

Make a group of six students. Next, have each group member choose a different topic from the box. Then find information about your topic. When you are ready, give a presentation to your group members about your topic.

Bigfoot	ghosts	reincarnation	UFOs	the Loch Ness Monster	vampires

My topic is vampires. I found three interesting things online about vampires. First, they can only survive by drinking blood. Second, they hate garlic. Finally, vampires can only enter a person's residence when invited in. I didn't believe in vampires before I began my research because the idea is silly, and I still hold on to that thought.

Have you ever seen a UFO?

Conversation

Listen and practice the conversation. 04-03

A Have you ever seen a UFO, Perry?

B Yes, I have. It happened a long time ago in a campground near my house in upstate New York.

A Tell me about it.

B My best friend and I used to go camping in the summers. On the last weekend in August, we were cooking hot dogs around a campfire when we looked up and saw these bright disks floating in the sky.

A What did you do?

B We were so dumbfounded that we couldn't move. We didn't even take out our phones for a picture. We just watched these objects for about thirty seconds and then they flew away.

A Were you scared?

B No, we were just amazed. In fact, we sat there watching them for so long that our hot dogs burned to a crisp.

Useful Expressions

A Let's learn about some verbs of perception.

see watch hear	
verb + object + present participle	**verb + object + infinitive (without *to*)**
I **saw** him **eating** a sandwich. My friend **watched** a movie **playing** in the theater. Marta **heard** the boy **teasing** the dog.	I **saw** him **perform** in the school play. Ben **watched** the tree **fall** from the strong winds. John **heard** the woman **scream**.

look taste touch feel smell
verb + object + present participle
We **looked** at the man **walking** toward the subway. Jeff **tasted** the hamburger **sitting** on the plate. My mom **touched** the soft blanket **sitting** on my bed. Carrie **felt** the dog **shaking** when she had finished giving it a bath. Elliot **smelled** the soup **cooking** in the pot.

B Fill in the blanks with the correct verb of perception.

1. Marianne ________ the robber running from her house with her own eyes.
2. Sam burned his hand when he ________ the plate sitting in the microwave.
3. I ________ the cat purring when I held it in my arms. It felt so sweet.
4. We ________ at the car driving on the wrong side of the road. We couldn't believe our eyes.
5. My dad ________ the cookies baking in the kitchen. He said, "What's that smell?"

Listening

A **Listen to the talk and choose True or False. If the statement is false, change it to make it true.** 04-04

1. Jiyoung spilled a drink on the kitchen counter.
2. Jiyoung witnessed five UFOs in the sky.
3. Jiyoung and her friend were talking on the balcony of her apartment.
4. Jiyoung and her friend watched the UFOs for a minute and a half.

B **Answer the questions with the correct information.**

1. What did Jiyoung see?
2. Where was Jiyoung?
3. What was Jiyoung doing at the time?
4. How did Jiyoung feel?

Speaking

Say what the most mysterious thing you have seen in your life is.

I saw a ghost in the basement of my house when I was 13. I was babysitting my younger brother, who was ten at the time. He wanted a toy from the basement but was scared to go down there by himself. So I went down there to get the toy and heard a strange sound. Out of the corner of my eye, I saw this apparition of a woman. She was floating about ten centimeters above the ground, and she looked so sad. I screamed and ran upstairs. I never went down there again!

Is there life on other planets?

Conversation

Listen and practice the conversation. 04-05

A Have you seen the movie *Contact*, John?
B Is that the one about space aliens?
A Yeah, that's right. It's based on a book by Carl Sagan.
B That was such an intelligent movie. The aliens teach the humans how to communicate with them.
A Do you think there's life on other planets?
B Do you mean intelligent life or just living organisms?
A Intelligent life.
B No, I don't think there's intelligent life out there. If there were, I feel like we would have communicated with them by now.
A How about living organisms?
B I feel like it's entirely possible a planet exists somewhere with living organisms on it. But I don't think we'll ever be able to prove it.

Group Work

Make a group of three students and choose one of the topics below. You and your group members' topics should be different. Read the articles relevant to your topic and answer the questions by using the information in the article. Then introduce your topic to your group members by using your answers.

The Bermuda Triangle | Atlantis | Area 51

The Bermuda Triangle is an area in the western region of the North Atlantic Ocean where ships and planes have disappeared under mysterious circumstances over the past 100 years. The region is thought to possess the supernatural ability to sink ships or down airplanes. Scientists reject that notion, however, insisting that extreme weather or other natural reasons are to blame for the missing ships and airplanes.

The lost island of **Atlantis** is an island mentioned in the writings of Plato in approximately 400 B.C. If the island existed, it was thought to have been located in the middle of the Atlantic Ocean. In Plato's writings, the island sank into the ocean approximately 9,000 years before his telling of the story. According to Plato, when the people of the island fell out of favor with the gods, the gods destroyed the island by submerging it deep into the ocean.

Area 51 is part of the United States military's Edwards Air Force Base and is located in a remote section of the Nevada desert. Some conspiracy theorists believe that an alien crashed its spacecraft on a ranch in Roswell, New Mexico, in 1947 and that the U.S. military transported the body of the alien and the wrecked spacecraft to a top-secret laboratory inside Area 51. The same conspiracy theorists believe that the U.S. military has made huge technological advances by studying the advanced technology on the alien spacecraft.

- What happened?
- When did it happen?
- Where did it happen?

Listening

A Listen to the two talks and answer the questions. 04-06

1-2

1. How big do the statues of Easter Island get?
   a. They get up to four meters in height and fourteen tons in weight.
   b. They get up to fourteen meters in height and four tons in weight.
   c. They get up to forty meters in height and fourteen tons in weight.
2. Why do alien theorists believe the statues were built?
   a. The natives of Easter Island built the statues so they would remember the aliens.
   b. The statues were a way for the inhabitants to honor the aliens.
   c. The statues were payment from the natives to the aliens for the knowledge that was shared.

3-4

3. Who do archaeologists think built Stonehenge?
   a. They think the Druids built Stonehenge.
   b. They think aliens built Stonehenge.
   c. They don't know who built Stonehenge.
4. Why do alien theorists think Stonehenge is circular?
   a. It is an arrival and departure site for alien spacecraft.
   b. The circle serves as the center of a map.
   c. The circle was important for the Druids'religious ceremonies.

B Complete the information about the ancient structures.

1.

Name ______________________

When was it built? ______________________

2.

Name ______________________

When was it built? ______________________

Speaking | Research an Unsolved Mystery

Research an unsolved mystery from your country. Answer the questions and share your answers with your classmates.

What is it?	
When did it occur?	
Where did it occur?	
What do you think really happened?	

The JFK assassination is an American mystery that is still discussed more than fifty years later. President John Kennedy was killed in Dallas, Texas, in 1963...

The Pyramids and Orion's Belt

Reading

A Read the article. 04-07

Archaeology Monthly

March 22nd, 2018

The Great Pyramids of Giza and Orion's Belt

Writer Jack Martinez

Each year, millions of tourists tolerate the scorching desert heat for the opportunity to visit one of the great wonders of the ancient world: the Pyramids of Giza. These breathtaking structures in the Egyptian desert were protective tombs for the mummified remains of Egyptian pharaohs. The ancient Egyptians believed that the proper preservation of a body after death was necessary for the afterlife. Since the discovery of the pharaohs' tombs, archaeologists have spent much of their time digging in and around the Great Pyramids in order to unearth ancient artifacts or evidence that tells them more about this ancient civilization. Although most archaeologists have focused their attention downward toward the earth and soil, one scientist's revelation concerning the Great Pyramids occurred while looking upward toward the sky. In 1983, Egyptologist Robert Bauval was gazing at the night sky with his family when he noticed something interesting in the Orion constellation. He realized that the three stars that make up Orion's belt were aligned in the same pattern as the three Great Pyramids of Giza. Many Egyptologists had found the slight misalignment of the Pyramids odd, but when compared to Orion's belt, it started to make sense to Bauval. A small group of scholars now believe that the Egyptians had designed the Great Pyramids to match the pattern of stars in Orion's belt. Of course, the Orion constellation is how we recognize that grouping of stars today, but what about during the time of the ancient Egyptians? They were also very familiar with that pattern of stars; however, the constellation was known to them as Osiris, the god of the underworld or judge of the dead. To have these tombs line up with that particular constellation is very interesting and may explain why the ancient Egyptians designed the Great Pyramids in that particular way.

Comprehension Check Answer the questions about the article.

1. Why were the dead bodies of the ancient Egyptians treated with special care?
2. Where do most archaeologists look for new information about the ancient Egyptians?
3. What interesting discovery did Robert Bauval make about the Great Pyramids?
4. What is the significance of the Osiris constellation?

B What do you think about the Orion Constellation theory? Is it plausible, or too fanciful?

Writing

In which place would you like to visit: the Great Pyramids of Egypt, Stonehenge, or Easter Island? Give reasons to support your answer.

Discussion

A Make a group of six to eight students. Divide the group into two groups and decide on each group's side: 1) agreeing with the statement or 2) disagreeing with the statement. Then discuss evidence and explanations that support your group's argument and take notes.

Does Life, Intelligent or Otherwise, Exist on Other Planets?

Group A	**Group B**
We agree with the statement because...	We disagree with the statement because...

B Now have a discussion with the group members from the opposing side.

I believe that life exists on other planets. I think the universe is just too big for it not to be true. We live on one planet in one solar system. But there are billions of stars, so that means there are billions of solar systems. Are you telling me that there isn't one other planet like ours that supports life? There has to be!

Wrap-up

A Complete the sentences with the correct vocabulary from the box.

Loch Ness Monster	Bigfoot	poltergeist	reincarnation	fortunetelling	Martians

1. The ____________ is thought to live in a lake in Scotland that bears the same name as the creature.
2. Although many photos of the Red Planet have been taken, no evidence of ____________ has been documented.
3. Another word for ghost is ____________.
4. ____________ is thought to be a large, hairy, apelike creature that supposedly lives in northern Canada.
5. Many people who practice the Hindu religion believe in ____________.
6. ____________ is still a popular practice in some parts of the world.

B Fill in the blanks with the correct verbs of perception: *look, feel, watch, smell, hear,* and *touch*.

1. Jonathon __________ the baseball float right over his glove and followed it with his eyes as it rolled all the way to the wall.
2. I __________ my phone vibrating in my pocket, but I couldn't answer it during the teacher's lecture.
3. We __________ at the painting hanging there for five minutes, but it never made sense to us.
4. My wife __________ the electric lamp, turning it on and off with only her fingertips.
5. Joe's grandpa __________ a pie baking in the oven. He said, "Do I smell apple pie?"
6. I thought I __________ a woman screaming in my neighborhood, so I called the police, but it was just a cat.

C Read the statement below. Think of reasons why both sides of the argument could be correct and take notes. Then choose a side and have a debate with a classmate. Take turns agreeing and disagreeing with the statement.

Although it is very expensive, humans need to colonize other planets to ensure the survival of our species.

I agree because...	I disagree because...

D Do you believe it is possible that ghosts or aliens actually exist, or are you a total skeptic when it comes to the paranormal?

Unit 5

Priorities

Warm-up

A Look at the post-it notes on the bulletin board and rank the four categories from one to four with one being the most important and four being the least important.

B Do you think this image correctly depicts the ways in which men and women prioritize things? If yes, what do you agree with? If no, what do you disagree with?

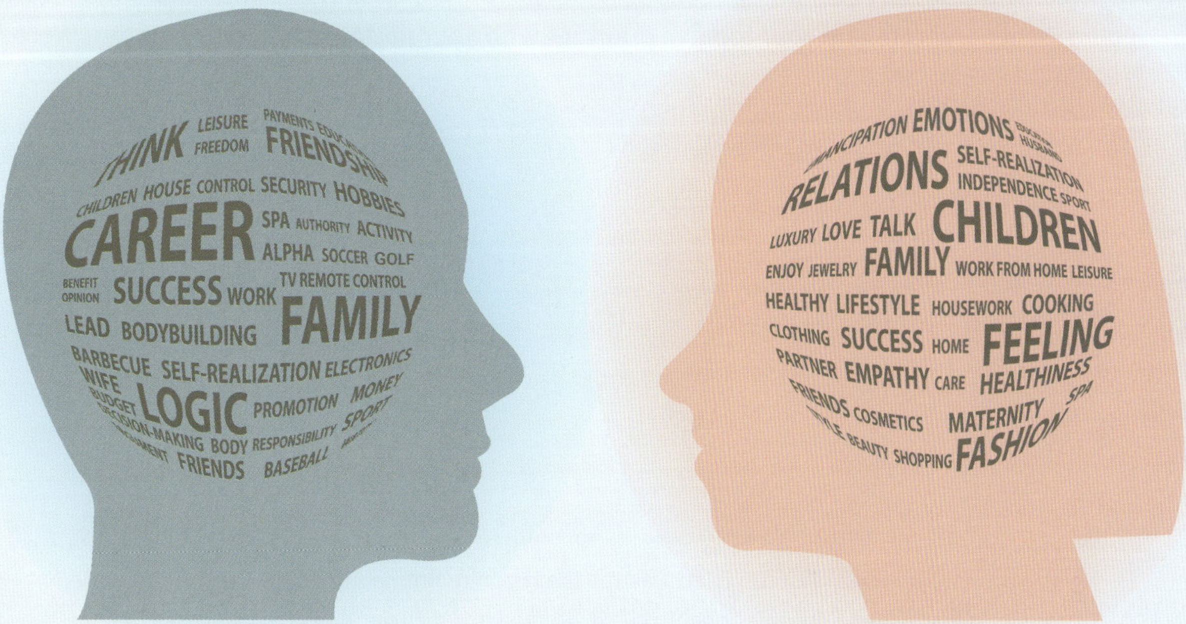

She thinks I work too much.

Conversation

Listen and practice the conversation. 05-01

A Can you believe this?

B I know. We have to stay late again to finish this quarter's numbers.

A My wife is going to kill me. She doesn't think I spend enough time at home.

B This job is demanding.

A She doesn't like that I hit golf balls after work either.

B You don't go home after work?

A I need to unwind. I usually hit golf balls for an hour at the driving range. Then, I go home.

B What about dinner with your family?

A I eat alone in the kitchen.

B I'd be angry too if I were your wife. I mean, what's more important, golf or your family? Well?

A I'm thinking.

B Ugh! You need to prioritize better.

TIPS & TIPS to unwind

to unwind = to relax, chill out, take a load off, take it easy, mellow out

I love to sit on the sofa at the end of a long day and watch my favorite television programs. It really helps me ***unwind****.*

Pair Work

Make a list of the top five priorities in your life. Use the following examples or create your own: family, health, career, relationships, school, hobbies, clothes, money, etc. Then share the list with your partner and compare your top five priorities with your partner's top five priorities. Were your answers similar?

1.
2.
3.
4.
5.

A What is your top priority?

B My top priority is health. You can't live a happy life if you're not healthy.

A I agree with you. Then, I put relationships next because my girlfriend is very important to me.

Listening

A Listen to the conversation and answer the questions. 05-02

1. What is the woman's problem?
   a. Her husband doesn't want to see a movie.
   b. She has to break her plans with a relative.
   c. She doesn't want to eat dinner with her boss.
2. When and where is the woman supposed to meet her sister?
   a. They're going to meet at half past eight in front of the theater.
   b. She and her sister are supposed to meet at nine thirty at a restaurant.
   c. They are going to meet at eight thirty in front of the ticket booth.
3. Why can't the woman do both activities?
   a. She has to work late.
   b. Both events take up too much time.
   c. The times of the two events conflict.
4. What do you think will happen next?
   a. The woman and her husband will enjoy a movie together.
   b. The man and the woman's sister will eat dinner with his boss.
   c. The man and the woman's sister will see the film *Heartbeats*.

B Listen again and change the false statements into true statements.

1. The woman's boss invited her and her husband to dinner.
2. The woman and her sister bought tickets at the theater.
3. The man is interested in dating the woman's friend.
4. The woman brought her husband to the Christmas party last year.

Pronunciation

A Let's learn some common reductions.

Common Reductions	
wanna: want to	What do you *wanna* do tonight?
wantsta: wants to	Benjamin asked, "Who *wantsta* go out for drinks after work?"
gonna: going to	Michael and Andre are *gonna* see a movie this weekend.
gotta: got to	Betty said, "My boyfriend's *gotta* get a real job. He's too old to be a D.J.!"
didja: did you	*Didja* have a good time at the museum?
hafta: have to	Ariel said, "I *hafta* be home by ten o'clock. My favorite show starts then."

*Reductions are NOT words and should never be written in formal documents.

B Say the sentences by using the proper reductions.

1. I've **got to** get up early tomorrow for a meeting.
2. **Did you** see the eclipse on Tuesday? It was amazing.
3. I don't **want to** be nosy, but are you still dating Craig McDaniels?
4. I **have to** say that this is the best Christmas party we've ever had!
5. Who **wants to** get a bite to eat after work?
6. I'm **going to** visit my parents in the city this weekend.

Here's what you should do.

Conversation

Listen and practice the conversation. 05-03

A Bernadette, could you help me prioritize these tasks? I don't want to bother Ms. Lippman again.
B Okay. What are you working on right now?
A Ms. Lippman is traveling to Hong Kong next week, so I need to book her a flight and make hotel reservations.
B Okay. And what else?
A I also need to process last month's travel expenses.
B Is that everything?
A Mr. Ryan asked me to write a newsletter reminding everyone about the company picnic next month.
B Okay, here's what you should do. The top priority is Ms. Lippman's travel plans. Book the flight and make the hotel reservations first. When that's finished, process those travel expenses. Employees hate waiting to be reimbursed. The last thing you should do is write the newsletter. That's the least pressing issue.
A Thank you so much, Bernadette. You're a real lifesaver!

Useful Expressions

A Look at the examples of common verb collocations.

book	prioritize	process	write
Lana, can you **book a table** for two tonight at Le Café?	Good workers learn how to **prioritize their duties**.	Eileen, can you **process this order**?	Can you wait a second? I have to **write** my boss **an email**.

B Complete the expressions by matching the correct phrase to the correct verb.

tasks   travel expenses   a newsletter   a hotel   a note   a flight   time   an application

1. book	2. prioritize	3. process	4. write

C Fill in the blanks to complete the talk.

A How's your day going Doris?
B I'm really busy, Mike. I have to __________ a number of job applications. Our company is hiring ten new workers this quarter. I also have to __________ a flight and a hotel room for Ms. Carson. She's going to a conference in Belgium next week. It's difficult to __________ tasks when there are so many important things to do at once. Oh no! I forgot to __________ Ms. Carson an email asking her if she wants a smoking or nonsmoking room.

Listening

A Listen to the woman's self-recording and answer the questions. 05-04

1. What is the topic of the morning meeting?
   a. They are talking about why the woman sent an email.
   b. They are discussing the cost projections for an office building in SoHo.
   c. They are talking about the price of building a hotel.

2. Why did the woman set up a lunch meeting?
   a. to discuss the construction of an indoor swimming pool in an expensive area of the city
   b. to discuss the zoning regulations and changes to existing design plans
   c. to discuss the addition of a parking lot in a site near a hotel entrance

3. Why does the woman need to speak to a lawyer about the office building project?
   a. She needs to discuss the laws concerning advertising near a subway station.
   b. She needs to talk about zoning regulations for the office building.
   c. She needs to discuss safety regulations regarding a project near a subway station.

4. What is she going to do with her friend?
   a. They're going to meet for coffee.
   b. They're going to have dinner together.
   c. They're going to meet for drinks.

B Complete the woman's to-do list.

To-Do List

8:00 a.m.	________ with Simon and Natasha
Lunchtime	meeting with Mr. Williams and ________
3:30 p.m.	meeting with ________
7:00 p.m.	________ with Janine
9:00 p.m.	________ SoHo report

Pair Work

To-Do List

A Make a to-do list for tomorrow. Start with the activities you have to do in the morning and finish with the things you need to do in the late evening.

To-Do List

Time	What You Have to Do

B Now share your to-do list with your partner. Who is busier? Who is less busy the next day?

I need a little more "me" time.

Conversation

Listen and practice the conversation. 05-05

A Mike, we need to talk.
B What's up, Melissa?
A You know I love spending time with you.
B I love spending time with you, too.
A But...
B Oh, no! Are you breaking up with me?
A No, it's nothing like that.
B Whew! What is it then?
A I just think we have been spending too much time together. We see each other every day, and I've stopped doing some of the things I enjoy.
B Like what?
A Like reading, meditating, and doing yoga. I know you don't like to do those things, and that's okay. I guess what I'm saying is that I need a little more "me" time.
B Okay, I understand. But we're still going to watch *Dragon Hunters* together on Sundays, right?
A Absolutely!

Discussion | Productive or Unproductive

A Make a group of four or five people. Then make a list of the ways your group members spend their alone time.

Ways We Spend Our Alone Time

reading, playing video games

B Now separate the list into two categories: productive or unproductive. Compare your two lists to your group members' two lists. Say why you chose to categorize them the way you did.

Productive	Unproductive
reading	*playing video games*

A I think reading books is productive because you can learn from books. But playing video games is a waste of time, so I put that in the unproductive category.
B I disagree. Playing video games improves your problem-solving skills, so I think it's productive.

Listening

A **Listen to the talk and answer the questions.** 05-06

1. What did the woman order at the coffee shop?
   a. She ordered a muffin and a café latte.
   b. She ordered a café latte and a piece of cake.
   c. She ordered a muffin and a chai tea latte.

2. What is true about the woman's visit to the spa?
   a. She left the spa when her massage was finished.
   b. She arrived just in time to make her appointment.
   c. She spent time using the spa facilities after her massage.

3. Why did the women have leftovers from the restaurant?
   a. The portion size of the meals was too large.
   b. They filled on up appetizers before the meal.
   c. They ordered too many dishes at the restaurant.

4. What can be inferred about the woman?
   a. She felt relaxed at the end of the day.
   b. Going home was stressful for her.
   c. She would have liked to stay at the bar longer.

B **Listen again and complete the information about what she did last Friday.**

What did she do last Friday?

Morning

Afternoon

Evening

Speaking | My Perfect Day

Think about your idea of the perfect day and describe it to your classmates in as much detail as possible.

My perfect day begins at about 9 a.m. when I wake up. I drink a delicious café latte from my favorite coffee shop and read the news on my smartphone. Then, I watch a movie at my local theater by myself. I stay home in the evening and order a pizza. I eat pizza, drink a bottle of my favorite beer, and listen to my favorite band, the Beatles. That's my perfect day!

It's as Simple as ABC!

Reading

A Read the article. 05-07

www.economytoday.com

It's as Simple as ABC!

Many years ago, when I was just a freshman in college, one of my college advisors shared with me a simple but profound practice that has worked well for me since I began using it all those years ago. This strategy worked when I was a nineteen-year-old college student, and it works for me now as a 55-year-old CEO of a fortune 500 company. I have experienced a lot of professional success in my life, and the effectiveness of this system deserves a large portion of the credit. My advisor called this system the ABCs of prioritizing, and I call it that, too.

The ABCs of prioritizing are simple, and they work like this. Not all work tasks and responsibilities are equal. Some things can wait while others cannot. The A stands for the A list, and this is the list of tasks that cannot wait. If you do not complete the tasks in list A, there will be serious consequences for you and your business. For example, if the most important client at your firm needs work to be completed by the afternoon and not completing it means you risk losing that client, then that is an A-list task. A-list tasks must be done now and supersede all other responsibilities. But be careful. If your A-list tasks are taking up more than 25% of your time, you are not prioritizing correctly.

B-list tasks should be those tasks that you spend most of your time doing. B-list tasks are not fires that need to be put out immediately. Instead, they are part of your regular work responsibilities. You will spend most of your time doing B-list tasks, and by doing them well, you will be on your way to achieving greatness. B list tasks are tasks where you have more time flexibility, and the deadlines are not as demanding as your A-list tasks. But don't confuse your B-list tasks with the last category, the C-list tasks.

C-list tasks are all of the other things you do during the workday that help you pass the time but do not advance your career. They could be lunch with a coworker, surfing the Internet, or organizing your stationery cabinet. They are things you might like to do, but putting them off will not negatively affect your career advancement. Spend little or no time on the C list. I mean, do you really need to get that cup of coffee with Roger and gossip about Betty, the new receptionist? Come on! Focus on the B list, tackle the A list as soon as something comes up, and pay little to no attention to the C list. I've done it this way for more than thirty years, and it has worked for me. It could work for you, too!

Comprehension Check Answer the questions about the article.

1. How did the author learn about the ABC system?
2. How long has the man used the system?
3. How does the man define A-list tasks?
4. What is the man's advice for a successful life and career?

B Is your system of prioritizing similar to the system outlined in the article?

Group Work

A Make a group of four students and ask them what their ABCs are with regard to their jobs or schools. Then take notes of your and your group members' answers.

	A List	B List	C List
Me			

B What are the two most popular answers for the ABCs? Choose a group representative and let him or her make a presentation about them.

We must (A).
We should (B).
(C) can wait until we...

Here are our ABCs. First, **we must** do our homework and study for exams. **We should** clean our dorm rooms and read our textbooks. Drinking coffee with friends and watching television **can wait until we** have some free time.

TIPS & TIPS *must, should,* and *can*

must (obligation): *If you win the lottery, you* ***must*** *buy your mother and father a new car.*
should (responsibility): *If you win the lottery, you* ***should*** *buy your mother and father a new car.*
can (possibility): *If you win the lottery, you* ***can*** *buy your mother and father a new car.*

Wrap-up

A Change the email from informal writing to formal writing by changing the five reductions to correctly spelled words.

> Dear Mr. Seung,
>
> I am writing this email because I wanna confirm our meeting for next week. I also hope your trip to China went well. Didja have a chance to meet with the factory manager? Do you think they will be able to manufacture our semiconductors for the amount we discussed? In our meeting next week, we hafta discuss the budget for our next project. I'm gonna bring my notes from my meeting with our U.S. client when we meet next week. I've gotta talk to Mr. Simmons in the U.S. office about some minor details regarding the new project before we meet. I'll let you know when I've spoken to Mr. Simmons.
>
> Sincerely,
>
> John Rand
> Project Manager of SB Corp.

B Write the correct verbs in the blanks: *book, prioritize, process,* and *write*.

1. My desk is full of notes. I really need to __________ these tasks.
2. Mary-jean, could you please __________ me a flight to New York?
3. I'm a little busy these days. I have to __________ these applications.
4. We should __________ a table for seven o'clock tomorrow.
5. Did you remember to __________ an email to Fran yesterday?
6. Gene and Kelly need to learn how to __________ their time more effectively.

C Read the list of tasks and put them into what you think are the appropriate categories. Then share your reasons for categorizing the tasks in that way with your partner.

- Go out to eat with your family
- Finish a report that is due tomorrow
- Vacuum the floor of your apartment or house
- Call your grandparents
- Get a haircut
- Return an urgent email from your boss

A	B	C

Unit
6
Genetics

Warm-up

A Write the names of the correct mixed-breed animals in the blanks 1 through 8. Then label each picture with the correct mixed-breed animal's name.

wholphin   grolar bear   beefalo   zebroid   liger   Savannah   cama   mule

1. bottlenose dolphin + killer whale = ________________
2. serval + domestic housecat = ________________
3. polar bear + grizzly bear = ________________
4. male camel + female llama = ________________
5. lion + tiger = ________________
6. zebra + horse = ________________
7. male donkey + female horse = ________________
8. cow + American bison = ________________

9. ________________

10. ________________

11. ________________

B Describe your sibling's appearance and personality. Who is he or she more similar to, your mother or your father? If you don't have any siblings, you can talk about one of your cousins.

My sister looks exactly like our mother. They share the same facial features. But my sister's personality is exactly like our father's personality. They're both introverts while my mother and I are both extroverts!

Am I losing my hair?

Conversation

Listen and practice the conversation. 06-01

A Honey, can I ask you a serious question?
B Sure, what is it?
A Am I losing my hair?
B No, of course not.
A Look at my comb. All of this hair came out.
B Turn around. Let me see the back.
A What is it? Am I balding?
B Your hair is thinning a bit in the back.
A Oh, no. I knew it! My dad's bald, and now I'm going bald, too. I've got bad genes!
B It's barely noticeable.
A Now. But what will it look like a year from now or five years from now?
B Why don't you take some medicine for it?
A Does it work?
B I heard there's a medicine you can take that will stop the balding process.
A Can I buy the medicine at the pharmacy?
B No, I think you need a doctor's prescription.

Words Search Puzzle

Find the words in the puzzle and circle them. Then match the words to the correct pictures.

clone offspring inherited laboratory embryo aging

1.

2.
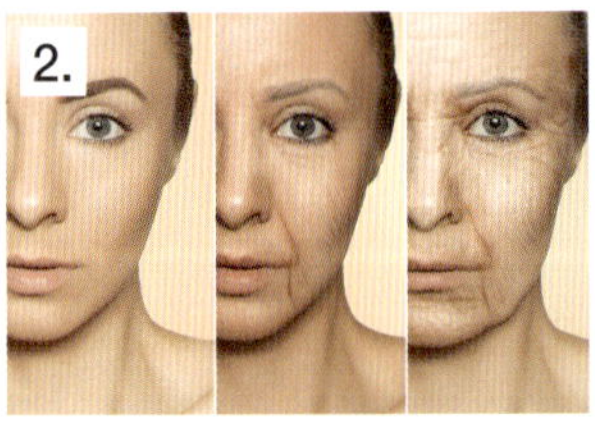

3.

s	s	l	x	q	w	s	d	g	i
o	p	a	o	r	g	a	n	s	n
f	o	b	g	u	y	j	o	c	h
f	e	o	a	g	i	n	g	f	e
s	m	r	w	d	c	l	q	s	r
p	b	a	y	a	j	i	n	a	i
r	r	t	k	c	l	o	n	e	t
i	y	o	k	l	r	q	s	a	e
n	o	r	s	c	d	n	a	c	d
g	a	y	f	f	s	c	y	x	a

4.

5.
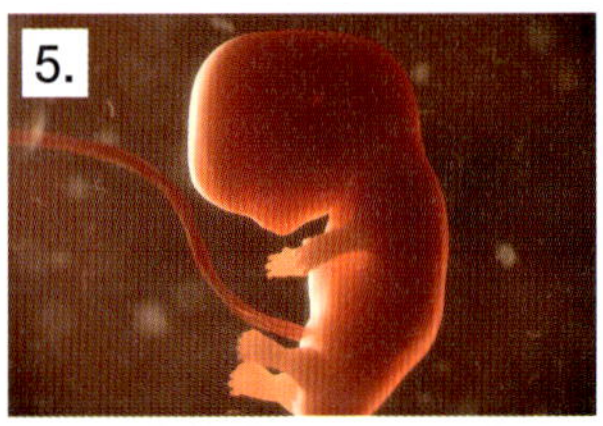

6.

Listening

A Listen to the conversation and change the false statements into true statements. 06-02

1. The woman thinks Pablo looks similar to his father.
2. Pablo is tall and has straight hair.
3. Amber looks more like her dad than her mom.
4. Amber thinks Marlene is the most beautiful of her sisters.
5. Tiffany and her husband have been married for three years.

B Label the couple's daughters with their correct names.

Amber Marlene Tiffany

father

mother

1.

2.

3.

Pair Work

Make a list of your mother's and father's physical and personality traits and make a list of the traits you have inherited from each of them. Then talk about your list with a partner.

Mother

Father

Me

A What traits have you inherited from your parents?
B I've got my mother's eyes and my father's dry sense of humor.

Designer Babies

Conversation

Listen and practice the conversation. 06-03

A Hey, Hyojin, how are things?
B Great, Chen. My sister just had a baby girl.
A Congratulations! You're an auntie.
B My sister and her husband had been trying for a couple years. Through the miracle of modern science, they were finally able to have a child.
A What do you mean by modern science?
B They used IVF. They got to choose the gender, too.
A Really? I didn't know that was possible.
B It's possible, but not all couples choose that option. A lot of couples like to be surprised.
A I see.
B IVF turned out to be a really positive thing for my sister.
A Why do you say that?
B My sister has always dreamed of having a little girl. Because of IVF, there was a one hundred-percent chance she would.

*IVF (in-vitro fertilization): the implantation of embryos into the womb

Useful Expressions

A Let's learn some useful expressions.

Asking for Clarification, Repetition, and Getting Someone's Attention	
A I've had a long day. I'm so tired. B **Pardon me?** It's so loud at this party. I couldn't hear you. A I said I was so tired. B Oh. Me, too!	A My boss is a real stickler for the rules. B **What do you mean by** stickler? A He's so strict. He gets mad if you're just one minute late. B That sounds terrible.
A **Excuse me.** B Oh, I'm sorry. A I just need to get past you. I'm going that way. B Oh, please go right ahead.	A It snowed a lot last night. Isn't it great? B **Why do you say that?** A They canceled school. We don't have to attend classes today. B Are you kidding? It's better than great!

B Complete the dialogues with the correct expressions.

1. A My boss criticized me yesterday. He said I wasn't diligent
   B ____________ diligent?
2. A ____________ I think you dropped your wallet. Is this yours?
   B Yes, it is. Thank you very much!

3. A I'm relieved attendance at the company picnic this weekend is optional.
   B ________________
   A I don't want to prepare anything.
   B Why don't you just buy something at the grocers?
   A ________________ I didn't hear you.
   B I said you could buy something at the grocery store.
   A Oh. I guess I could do that.

Listening

Listen to the interview and answer the questions. 06-04

1. According to the doctor, what is a benefit of having a designer baby?
   a. The baby will definitely have a healthy life.
   b. The baby will receive the parents' best traits.
   c. The baby will grow up to be a great athlete.
2. What does the doctor say about people's understanding of genetic modification?
   a. People are very aware of what is possible and not possible.
   b. Scientists are capable of much more than people realize.
   c. People's expectations are unrealistic with regard to what's possible now.
3. Why does the doctor say it is difficult to modify a human embryo?
   a. There are too many steps in the process of genetically modifying a human embryo.
   b. Modifying human embryos is in its infancy and is too expensive to research.
   c. Human embryos contain so many genes that it becomes very difficult to change only one.
4. What can scientists do now with regard to genetically modifying human embryos?
   a. They can alter the genetic structure of an embryo after implantation.
   b. They can test embryos for the ones with the best traits and implant them.
   c. They can implant embryos and then test them for the best genetic traits.

Class Activity | Ranking the Traits

A Look at the list of genetic traits and rank them in order of importance from 1 to 5 with 1 being the most important and 5 being the least important to you.

Physical Attractiveness ☐ High IQ ☐ Good Health ☐

Athletic Ability ☐ Good Personality ☐

B Now the teacher will take a vote by reading each category aloud. Raise your hand when you hear the teacher read your number-one most important category. Which genetic trait received the most and the least votes?

Stem Cell Therapy

Conversation

Listen and practice the conversation. 06-05

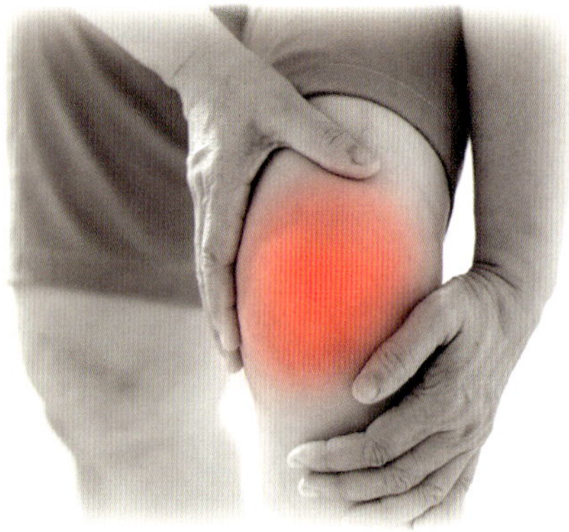

A Hey, Paul. How was your doctor's appointment?

B Not so good, Jack.

A What did the doctor say?

B He ran some tests on my knee. I have arthritis.

A What can he do about it?

B Not much. He said he can treat the symptoms, but he can't cure the arthritis.

A I read an interesting article about stem cell therapy last week.

B I thought stem cell therapy was just a scam.

A No, it's real. The treatment is just in its early stages now. The article mentioned a runner with an arthritic knee who felt much better after receiving stem cell injections in the injured knee.

B Hmm. Maybe I'll check it out. Thanks for the advice.

*stem cell therapy: the use of stem cells to heal and repair damaged cells in the body

TIPS & TIPS ~ therapy

Do you think ***stem cell therapy*** *works?*
Jin went to the clinic for some ***physical therapy****.*
Marianne bought these scented candles. They're great for ***aromatherapy****.*
Justin overcame his speech disorder by receiving ***speech therapy****.*

Vocabulary

Look at the list of illnesses. Then write the names of the illnesses in your native language and English definitions. Use a dictionary if necessary.

1. Alzheimer's

2. Parkinson's

3. Diabetes

4. Arthritis

5. Multiple Sclerosis (MS)

6. Lupus

7. Kidney Disease

8. Liver Disease

9. Stroke

10. Heart Conditions

Listening

A Listen to the talk and answer the questions. 06-06

1. What two problems regarding transplants are discussed in the talk?
   a. long waiting lists and transplant rejection
   b. transplant rejection and the high cost of surgery
   c. the high cost of surgery and long waiting lists

2. How many transplants are performed annually in the United States?
   a. fewer than 3,000
   b. over 30,000
   c. more than 300,000

3. What are the benefits of growing an organ for transplant in a laboratory?
   a. It's cheaper and easier than harvesting an organ.
   b. Patients will move up the waiting lists more quickly.
   c. Doctors will become more proficient at surgery.

4. What can we infer about a future where organs are grown in laboratories?
   a. More people will be in need of organs.
   b. People will have longer life expectancies.
   c. More people will be willing to donate organs.

B Discuss the following questions related to the talk.

1. If scientists can soon grow human organs in a laboratory, what other applications do you think this kind of medical technology offers?
2. Do you think science will allow us to have average life expectancies of 100 years or more?
3. Scientists are currently trying to grow meat in laboratories. If successful, it would eliminate the need to kill animals for their meat. Would you eat lab-grown animal meat? Why or why not?

Medical Breakthroughs

A Look at the list of interesting medical breakthroughs that could be on the horizon. Discuss the ones you believe to be the most important. Why do you think so?

- a cure for cancer
- a treatment to determine skin tone or hair color
- a cure for degenerative brain diseases such as Alzheimer's or Parkinson's
- a cure for male-pattern baldness
- a cure for blindness
- a treatment to determine height
- a treatment to prevent obesity or weight problems
- a cure for deafness
- a treatment to determine body shape or facial features

B What other medical breakthrough would you like to see in the near future?

A What medical breakthrough would you like to see in the near future, Alice?

B I believe a cure for brain disease would be one of the most important breakthroughs in medicine. Dementia and memory loss are two of the horrible symptoms related to brain disease.

Are You a Super-Sleeper?

Reading

Read the article. 06-07

Are You a Super-Sleeper?

For most of us, fewer than eight hours of sleep per night results in our feeling groggy, grumpy, or even anxious the next day. For a lucky few, however, surviving on fewer than six hours of sleep per night is not a problem. Scientists have actually discovered a gene, the DEC2 mutation, which allows certain people to become short-sleepers. A short-sleeper is a person who can get by on six or fewer hours of sleep per night and feel no negative effects the following day.

Regular sleepers, like me, need eight hours of sleep per night. Just ask my husband! Chronic lack of sleep is linked to a number of health problems, such as high blood pressure, strokes, and heart attacks. The body's ability to repair itself on the cellular level strongly correlates to the amount of quality sleep one gets. A good night's sleep helps us perform well physically and cognitively and keeps our immune system robust.

Why are these lucky few able to survive on such limited sleep, you might ask? The answer lies in the quality of the sleep they are getting. My new smartphone has a fast-charging option that my old phone did not have. It can charge to 100% capacity in a fraction of the amount of time it took my older-generation phone to achieve. Scientists believe short-sleepers are actually super-sleepers in that they possess the ability to access deeper REM states. Super-sleepers are able to achieve adequate levels of restfulness, but in smaller segments of time.

The old expression "quality over quantity" may actually apply to the way we sleep, too. Unfortunately, not all of us are lucky enough to have access to this more efficient form of slumber. Right now, it is reserved for those lucky few with the DEC2 mutation. Perhaps in the near future, scientists will find a way to share this mutation with the rest of us. They could end up creating an even more productive version of human being or at least a version with a couple of extra hours each day to tidy up around the house or to surf the Internet.

Comprehension Check Answer the questions about the article.

1. Approximately how much sleep does a short-sleeper require per night?
2. Why are short-sleepers able to thrive on less sleep?
3. What are some problems associated with a chronic lack of sleep?
4. What do scientists think the DEC2 gene does?
5. What does the author think might happen in the near future?

Writing

Write a short essay about your genetic gifts. What kind of interesting traits have you inherited from your parents?

Writing a Report

Read the paragraph about cloning. Then complete the report below.

There is quite a debate occurring in the scientific community these days regarding human cloning. Although human cloning has the potential to be dangerous and unethical, it could also help doctors save countless peoples' lives. There are two versions of cloning being researched right now. The first is reproductive cloning. This is the version where one organism is copied using DNA from the original organism. At this time, most nations have decided that reproductive cloning in humans is unethical and that it should be illegal. The second type of cloning is called therapeutic cloning, and it has given patients with organ failure new hope. Therapeutic cloning involves the use of stem cells in order to grow parts of a person's body such as the kidney, liver, or heart. When the organs reach full maturity, they can be transplanted into the body of the sick person. The organs will be perfect matches for the recipients because they will be grown in a lab using the recipient's DNA. This second type of cloning is being thoroughly researched and may become one of the most important medical breakthroughs in decades.

The Cloning Debate

This article discusses cloning. The writer describes two versions of cloning. The first is called __________ cloning. It involves ______________________________.

The second type of cloning is __________ cloning. It involves ______________________________.

A benefit of therapeutic cloning is that ______________________________.

Therapeutic cloning may become the most important medical breakthrough in decades.

Wrap-up

A Fill in the blanks with the correct words from the word box.

clone   offspring   inherited gene   DNA   embryo   aging

1. Dolly the sheep was a __________ of another sheep. She is the first animal to be genetically copied from the cells of another.
2. My dog had a litter of seven __________. There were three males and four females.
3. Scientists hope to implant a mammoth __________ into an Asian elephant's uterus.
4. We can learn about our own ancestry by using __________ testing, but testing is expensive.
5. Anti-__________ cream is a very popular cosmetic product.
6. I started going bald at a young age. This was due to an __________ from my father. He's bald, too.

B Complete the dialogues with the expressions: *Excuse me., Pardon me?, What do you mean by ~?,* and *Why do you say that?*

1. A __________________ Could you move over one chair? My friend is coming.
   B Why do I have to move?
   A __________________
   B Why do I have to move? I was here first.
   A Okay, fine. Never mind. I'll find a different seat.

2. A Isn't the holiday season stressful?
   B __________________ I love Thanksgiving and Christmas. The time we get to spend with family is worth it!

3. A Our project in biology is DOA.
   B __________________ DOA?
   A It's dead on arrival.

C Interview a classmate about the genetics questions.

	Answers
1. Do you look like your mother or father?	
2. Who does your mother look like: your grandmother or grandfather?	
3. How about your father?	
4. What similarities in personality do you share with your siblings?	
5. Are there any strange habits you share with family members?	

D If you could change something about your genetic make up, what would you change (height, hair color, athleticism, etc)?

Unit
7
Personal Finance

Warm-up

A Look at the pictures and say what each person's financial situation is.

Allen's personal finances are a mess. He always spends his paychecks on frivolous things and doesn't save a dime. When his checking account is empty, he uses his credit cards. Now he has a lot of credit card debt. He's two months behind on his gas bill, three months behind on his electric bill, and a month behind on his rent.

Allie is the opposite of her brother Allen. Her personal finances are always in order. She's caught up on her rent as well as her other bills. She puts one-fourth of her monthly paychecks into her savings account, and she only buys things she really needs. She has one credit card, but she pays off the balance at the end of each month.

B Which person's financial situation most accurately describes your own?

What is the asking price?

Conversation

Listen and practice the conversation. 07-01

A Okay, let's crunch these numbers one more time.
B All right. What do you want to know?
A What is the asking price?
B They want $320,000 for it, but they are willing to come down to $300,000.
A Okay. And how much is the down payment?
B It's 10%, so we need to come up with $30,000.
A Thirty grand, huh? That's a lot.
B I know, but I really love this house.
A Me, too. So our mortgage will be $270,000?
B That's right. But it's a 30-year fixed-rate mortgage.
A It's a fixed-rate mortgage? I thought it was an ARM.
B No, it's a fixed-rate mortgage at 3.2%. The low rate is part of a government subsidy for first-time homebuyers.
A Okay. Let's do it.

*ARM: adjustable rate mortgage

Vocabulary | Purchasing a Home

A Read the definitions and write the words in the correct places.

adjustable rate mortgage　government subsidy　fixed rate mortgage
mortgage　crunch numbers　asking price

1. ________________ a loan for a house or apartment
2. ________________ an interest rate that does not increase or decrease over time
3. ________________ an interest rate that fluctuates in relation to the health of the economy
4. ________________ the price an owner of a house or an apartment wants to be paid before negotiating begins
5. ________________ money from the government to help pay for something
6. ________________ to compute or calculate a series of numbers

B Have you ever taken out a large loan for a house or a car? If yes, how large was the loan you took out?

Listening

A Listen to the conversation and change the false statements into true statements. 07-02

1. The man is interested in buying a new motorcycle.
2. The man is applying for a large personal loan.
3. The man and his wife own a house and an apartment.
4. The branch manager won't approve the man's loan.

B Listen again and complete the information card.

Personal Debt:

Requested Loan Amount:

Credit Rating: □ excellent □ good □ fair □ poor □ other

Loan Officer's Decision: □ approved □ denied

Pair Work

Complete the table by using one of the situation cards below and role-playing a conversation. Take turns being the loan officer and the customer.

Loan Officer	Customer
Welcome to 1st National Bank. How may I help you today?	Hello. My name is ______________, and I'd like to apply for a loan.
What do you do for living?	I am a/an ______________.
What kind of loan are you seeking?	□ a student loan □ a car loan □ a mortgage □ a personal loan □ a business loan
How much would you like to borrow?	□ $100,000+ □ $50,000 - $100,000 □ $10,000 - $50,000 □ $10,000-
What amount of personal debt do you have?	□ $50,000 - $100,000 □ $10,000 - $50,000 □ $10,000- □ none
How is your credit?	□ excellent □ good □ fair □ poor □ other
Approved	Congratulations! You have been approved for the loan.
Denied	I'm really sorry, but I'm afraid we can't offer you a loan because...

Situation 1	Situation 2	Situation 3	Situation 4	Situation 5
Bill Mitchell	Virginia Chang	Janine Kim	Anthony Watkins	Lily Sanderson
small business owner	student	engineer	police officer	taxi driver
business loan / $89,000	student loan / $30,000	mortgage / $175,000	personal loan (boat) / $5,000	car loan / $11,000
-$27,000	$0.00	-$32,000	-$55,000	-$3,000
good	no credit history	excellent	poor	fair

A Welcome to 1st National Bank. How may I help you today?
B Hello. My name is Bill Mitchell, and I'd like to apply for a loan.

Credit Card Debt

Conversation

Listen and practice the conversation. 07-03

A Mom, can you take a look at my credit card statement? I don't know what this number means.

B Let me see. This is your balance.

A Then what is this number here?

B That's your minimum payment due.

A What does that mean?

B It means you have to pay at least that much in order to avoid paying any penalties.

A What if I can't make the payment?

B Then the credit card company will charge you an extra amount.

A How much will it charge me?

B I don't know. There are different terms for different credit cards. Because you're a new cardholder, I assume the penalties are rather high.

A I owe $220 this month, but I can only pay $150. Will you and Dad help me with the rest?

B We'll help you this month, but you need to budget your money better. You're twenty years old. You're an adult. You need to start acting responsibly.

Vocabulary | Credit Cards

Put the words in the correct places.

credit card company   interest rate   credit card statement

magnetic strip   credit card number   credit card reader

1.

2.

3.

4.

5.

6.

Listening

A Listen to the conversation and answer the questions. 07-04

1. What does the woman think the man's problem is?
   a. He spends too much money on unnecessary things.
   b. He ordered too many credit cards from credit card companies.
   c. He is paying too much interest on his current credit cards.

2. Which of the following statements is true?
   a. Half of the man's monthly salary goes toward his credit card debt.
   b. A majority of his monthly salary goes toward his credit card debt.
   c. About a third of his salary goes toward his credit card debt.

3. What can be inferred about the man's relationship with his sister?
   a. They don't get along very well.
   b. He values her financial advice.
   c. He often borrows money from her.

B Listen again and fill in the blanks with the correct information.

Cardholder's Name: *Mr. Daniel S. Fullerton*
Number of Credit Cards:
Amount of Debt:
Minimum Monthly Payments Due:

Pair Work

A Complete the questionnaire that applies to you and share the result with your partner.

Do you have any credit cards? If your answer is no, skip to 5.

1. How many credit cards do you have?
2. What have you most recently purchased by using your credit card?
3. What benefits, if any, do you receive by using your credit card?
   □ cash back □ loyalty points □ special discounts □ building a credit history □ air miles □ other (__________)
4. Is there a particular credit card company that you would recommend? If yes, which one?
5. Why haven't you applied for a credit card?
   □ prefer cash or debit □ bad credit □ fear of losing the card □ fear of identity theft □ don't know how to apply
   □ no job / no income □ other (__________)
6. Do you want to apply for a credit card in the near future? If yes, why do you want to do so?
   □ convenient □ to build a credit history □ special discounts □ cash back □ loyalty points □ air miles
   □ other (__________)
7. When do you feel like you wish you had a credit card?
   □ shopping □ socializing with friends □ unexpected expenditures □ traveling □ no ATMs nearby
   □ when carrying lots of cash □ other (__________)

B Talk with your partner about the upside and downside of using credit cards.

Should I cosign the loan?

Conversation

Listen and practice the conversation. 07-05

A Honey, can we talk?
B Sure, what's going on?
A Shingo asked me to cosign a loan.
B How much is the loan for?
A $25,000.
B No way! It's too much.
A I know, but he really needs the money. He wants to start a business.
B Then he should ask his parents or another relative.
A But he's my best friend. Don't you think I owe him this favor?
B No, I don't. If he doesn't repay the loan, we're on the hook for it.
A I know.
B What's the business idea?
A He wants to start a noodle restaurant downtown. He's got a spot picked out and everything.
B I'm sorry, Jim, but it's too risky.
A You're right. I just hope he's able to get the money somehow.

*on the hook for = responsible for

Grammar

A Let's learn about the verbs *hope* and *wish*.

We use **hope** to talk about an outcome we desire in the future. **hope + (noun clause)** I hope (that) he wins the race.	We use **wish** to talk about an outcome we desire in the future but is not possible. **wish + (noun clause)** I wish (that) I had a nicer car.
I **hope** that Minsuk is on time for the meeting. (present) Jerry **hopes** his brother does well on the college entrance exam this fall. (future) Shinzo **hopes** that his wife's first day of work went well. (past)	1. *were* = a present hypothetical condition I **wish** that it weren't raining today, so we could go to the beach. Jeanie **wishes** she were taller. 2. *were going to* = a future hypothetical condition Sam and Raquel **wish** that they were going to go to Hawaii this winter. 3. *had* + past participle = a past hypothetical condition Carla **wishes** she had studied harder in high school.

*We use *hope* when the result of a past action is unknown.

B Complete the sentences with the correct forms of the verbs *hope* and *wish*.

1. I ________ the weather is nice this Sunday, so we can have our picnic.
2. I ________ I had learned to play the guitar when I was younger.

3. Hyobin ________ that he were attending the concert this Friday.

4. Geraldine ________ her favorite politician wins the election.

5. Ray ________ he would have majored in economics instead of engineering.

Listening

A **Listen to the radio show and answer the questions.** 07-06

1. What is NOT true about the show *Truth Talk*?
   a. The audience members receive free financial advice.
   b. The callers can also be audience members of the show.
   c. The show provides listeners with loans to pay off debts.

2. What does Mira think the couple should pay off last?
   a. credit cards b. house c. car

3. What can be inferred about Mira Swanson?
   a. She went to school to study broadcasting.
   b. She became a broadcaster because of her experience in finance.
   c. She owned her own financial institution before becoming a broadcaster.

4. What can be inferred about the couple?
   a. Poor spending practices slowed their ability to pay off loans.
   b. They tried hard to pay down their mortgage quickly.
   c. The woman's monthly salary is more than the man's.

5. What do you think the couple will do?
   a. They will pay off their credit cards first.
   b. They will go shopping for a new car.
   c. They will sell their house and move.

B **Listen again and complete Mr. and Mrs. Lee's debt summary.**

✓ Current Mortgage Balance:
✓ Credit Cards:
✓ Car Debt:
Total Debt:

Establishing a Good Credit History

Put a check next to the examples that would help you to establish a good credit history.

☐ Apply for a credit card with a low credit limit. Then, pay the balance off in full each month.
☐ Pay only the minimum balance each month on your credit cards.
☐ Miss a payment or two on your loans.
☐ Take out a loan and then pay it back in the proper amount of time.
☐ Only use cash, so there's no record of your purchases.
☐ Buy a house and make your mortgage payments on time.

Dear Mom and Dad

Reading

A Read the letter. 07-07

Dear Mom and Dad,

I'm writing this letter to you because I have had a string of bad luck recently, and I need to ask you for a favor. You see, last week, my car started making some strange sounds. I wasn't sure what the problem was, so I brought it to a mechanic. The mechanic told me that the timing belt needed to be replaced, and while he was doing an overall check of the vehicle, he told me that my brake pads also needed to be replaced. Then, when he moved my car, he noticed that oil had leaked on the ground. Yep, you guessed it. My car was also leaking oil. The total bill for all of the parts and labor was $975. If that wasn't bad enough, the next day my roommate told me that she was moving out of the apartment immediately. A friend of hers from high school recently moved to town, and she wants to live with her. I told her I couldn't cover the rent without her help, but she didn't really seem to care. Since my name is on the lease and not hers, she is free to leave whenever she pleases, and there's nothing I can do about it. Our rent is $1,400 a month, so now I have to cover an additional $700 I wasn't expecting. You probably think that my sad story is finished, but it's not. The day after my roommate told me she was moving out, my manager notified me that I was being laid off from my job at the insurance company due to downsizing. The company didn't offer me much of an exit package. I will receive two weeks' pay, and that's it. I've already begun looking for another job, but the job market is tough out here on the West Coast. A friend of mine at Infinity Insurance agreed to hire me next month, but the new job there only pays about 75% of what my old job paid. Right now, I have $1,500 in my bank account, but my rent is due next week. I put the car repairs on my credit card, so my credit card balance is $2,500 now. I wonder if you guys would be willing to lend me $5,000. Once I'm back on my feet, I will come up with a repayment plan, I promise.

Love,

Cassandra

P.S. Happy birthday, Mom! I hope you got my e-card. I'm sorry I couldn't afford to send a real one.

Comprehension Check Answer the questions about the letter.

1. What financial problems is Cassandra experiencing right now?
2. Why did Cassandra initially bring her car to the mechanic?
3. Why was Cassandra's roommate able to move out any time she pleased?
4. What's the downside of Cassandra's new job?
5. How do you think Cassandra will feel if her parents agree to give her the money?

B What would you do if your son or daughter wrote you a letter like this?

Group Work

A Imagine you are having financial problems and need to borrow money from a relative or friend. Write a letter asking to borrow some money and the reason why you need to borrow the money. Use one of the problems from the table.

Savings Account: $300

Problems Check the option you want to mention in the letter as your problem.	□ need new car engine / $2,000 □ monthly rent due / $900 □ credit card / $500 □ university tuition / $1,300

Dear ______________________,

____

____

____

____

____

Love,

____

B Read your letter to your group members. Then, as a group, choose the most convincing letter and reply to it by accepting or declining the request.

Dear ______________________,

____

____

____

____

____

Love,

____

C Did you accept or decline the request? Share your reply with your group members.

Wrap-up

A Fill in the blanks with the correct words from the word box.

mortgage	interest rate	credit card statement
credit card number	credit card reader	crunch

1. Mr. and Mrs. Chen's monthly ________________ payment for their house is $1,400.
2. The ________________ on my car loan is 4.5%.
3. In order to purchase something online, you have to input your ________________.
4. Look at this ________________! You bought a new stereo without telling me?
5. Paulo is going to ________________ the numbers before he and his wife decide to buy a house.
6. The pizza deliveryman ran the man's card through the ________________.

B Complete the sentences with the correct forms of the verbs *hope* and *wish*.

1. Jim ____________ he knew more people in town. He gets bored on weekends.
2. Wendy ____________ that she gets the job as a flight attendant. She would love to travel the world.
3. Isabelle ____________ her sister isn't stuck in traffic right now. The concert starts at seven o'clock.
4. Do you ____________ you grew up in a different city?
5. The teacher ____________ her students attended classes more regularly.

C Make a list of all the pros and cons regarding borrowing money.

Pros

You can start a business.

Cons

You have to pay interest.

D Who taught you how to manage your money? What financial rules do you live by?

Unit 8

Emergencies

Warm-up

Look at the pictures and say what happened in each picture.

1.

2.

3.

4.

5.

6.

I smell smoke.

Conversation

Listen and practice the conversation. 08-01

A Do you smell smoke?
B Yes, I do.
A Look! I see smoke rising from over there.
B Should I call 911?
A I hear sirens. I think they're already on their way.
B Which building is it?
A I think it's coming from that office building on 1st Street.
B Do you think everyone's okay?
A It's Sunday, so no one should be working there today.
B That's true. I'm going to go inside and turn on the news.
A Good idea. Maybe they're doing a live report of the incident.

Vocabulary | Emergencies

Match the words with the correct definitions.

1. unconscious •	• a. death or injury by electricity
2. choking •	• b. a bruise on the skin
3. a stroke •	• c. swelling around the brain due to being hit in the head
4. shallow breathing •	• d. weakly inhaling and exhaling due to injury or illness
5. emergency room (ER) •	• e. an obstruction in the airway that prevents oxygen from entering the lungs
6. an ambulance •	• f. a vehicle used to transport injured people to the hospital
7. a concussion •	• g. the loss of oxygen to the brain due to a lack of blood flowing through the arteries
8. electrocution •	• h. the inability to stay awake or aware
9. a contusion •	• i. the area of the hospital that treats patients who are in the most serious condition

Listening

A Listen to the conversation and answer the questions. 08-02

1. What is the problem with the woman's phone?
   a. It caught on fire in her pocket.
   b. Her phone model has been recalled.
   c. The battery life is very short.

2. How long did the woman own the PR5?
   a. She had it for eighteen months.
   b. She had it for a year.
   c. She had it for a year and a month.

3. What can we infer about the company that makes the PR6?
   a. It will not give full refunds.
   b. It will lose a lot of money.
   c. It will recall the PR5 phone, too.

4. What do you think will happen next?
   a. The woman will take the phone back to the shop.
   b. The woman will keep the phone anyway.
   c. The man will purchase the phone from the woman for a discount.

B Listen again and choose True or False.

1. The woman has just bought the newest model of phone. [True / False]
2. The man told her she would lose her $700. [True / False]
3. If the PR6 malfunctions, it will not cause bodily harm. [True / False]
4. The woman plans to exchange her phone or get a refund. [True / False]

Pair Work

To-Do List

A Read the following questions. Then check the correct boxes.

Do you know anyone who has		
	witnessed a fire?	□ yes □ no
	been in an accident?	□ yes □ no
	spent the night in the hospital?	□ yes □ no
	had surgery?	□ yes □ no
	helped someone in an emergency?	□ yes □ no
	ridden in an ambulance?	□ yes □ no
	visited an ER?	□ yes □ no

B Was there a question you said yes to? Discuss that question in more detail with your partner.

Somebody call 911!

Conversation

Listen and practice the conversation. 08-03

A Marco, are you all right?

B I'm not sure, Sheila. I don't feel very well.

A You look pale. Are you in pain?

B Yes. My chest feels really tight.

A I'm calling 911.

B No, wait. It's probably nothing.

A No, Marco. We're not going to take any chances. I'm calling the paramedics now.

B Okay.

911 Emergency Services. What's your emergency?

A My coworker might be having a heart attack. We need an ambulance immediately.

911 What's your location?

A We're at the Smithson Building on the 32nd floor.

911 Okay, the paramedics are on their way right now.

Pair Work Use the cards in order to role-play an emergency telephone conversation with your partner. Take turns being the operator and the caller.

1

Type of Emergency: a large fire in the warehouse across the street

Location: 121 Penny Drive, Dayton, Ohio

Description: You were working in a building across the street when you heard an explosion. Then, you saw smoke and flames coming out of the windows of the warehouse. It's still burning!

2

Type of Emergency: a robbery

Location: Lee's Liquor Shop, 4848 Jackson Avenue, Omaha, Nebraska

Description: A man in a black ski mask just robbed you at gunpoint. You were the only clerk working in the store when the robbery occurred.

Listening

A Listen to the talk and answers the questions. 08-04

1. Who is Walter Peterson talking to?
   a. He's talking to heart attack survivors.
   b. He's talking to doctors and nurses.
   c. He's talking to emergency medical technicians.
2. What symptoms did Walter experience before his heart attack?
   a. He had shoulder pain and a stomachache.
   b. He had arm and shoulder pain.
   c. He had a headache and shoulder pain.
3. What did Walter do to treat his symptoms?
   a. He massaged his shoulder muscles.
   b. He took some pills for the pain.
   c. He stopped working and got some rest.
4. Why did Walter give this talk?
   a. He wanted to help other people who might be at risk of heart attacks.
   b. He wanted to give helpful information to EMTs about how to do their jobs better.
   c. He wanted to thank the EMTs for helping him during his medical emergency.
5. What do you think can be inferred about Walter?
   a. He changed his lifestyle because of this experience.
   b. He didn't want to do any more gardening because of his heart attack.
   c. He's afraid to exercise because of this medical emergency.

B Listen again and complete the information.

Walter Peterson

Medical Condition:

EMT Response Time:

Who did what: Julia or Kim?

Did Chest Compressions:

Gave Oxygen:

Walter's Recovery Time:

Making a List

Research some ways a person can avoid suffering from a heart attack or stroke later in life. Make a list of the things a person can start doing right now. Then share them with your group members.

List of Changes

- *quit smoking*
- *exercise daily*
-
-
-
-

This is a fire drill!

Announcement

Listen and practice the announcement. 08-05

Okay, everyone, this is just a fire drill. I need everyone to move toward the office emergency exit doors. I need you to move in an orderly fashion. Please don't push or shove. Just walk briskly toward the exit doors. Now, in a single file line, I want you to move down the staircase to the ground floor and then exit the building. You must not use the elevator. This is a fire drill, so there's no need to panic. I need you to move in a single file line down the staircase and then out of the office. Once outside, you need to continue walking through the parking lot. I need everyone to be at least 200 meters from the building. I repeat: you need to be a minimum of 200 meters away from the building. An area in the parking lot has been cleared for workers. Go to the area that has been cleared for office workers. Thank you!

Grammar

A Let's learn about infinitives as objective complements.

verb + object + infinitive (complement)
I **need you to call** Raymond immediately to tell him tomorrow's meeting is canceled.
Our professor **wants us to decide** on a topic for our group presentation by Wednesday.
Lily **persuaded Alex to go** on a hike even though he doesn't care for the outdoors.
The doctor **encouraged his patient to exercise** more and **to lose** some weight.
The loud thunderstorm **caused the dog to run** under the sofa and not **to come** out.
Jenny's parents **would like everyone to know** that Jenny's surgery went well and that Jenny will make a full recovery.
Our parents **got us to clean** the garage by promising us $20 each when we finish.

B Put the sentences in the correct order.

1. the assignment. / to give him / an extra week / He finally persuaded / to hand in / the teacher

____

2. My trainer / to work hard / encourages me / during our / training sessions.

____

3. the airport. / Minsoo would / to meet / like you / him at

____

4. to slow / The snow / down immensely. / caused traffic

____

5. remain / everyone / We / to / calm! / need

____

Listening

A **Listen to the announcement and answer the questions.** 08-06

1. Why is the woman talking to the office workers?
   a. She is telling them about the emergency escape plan she has created.
   b. She is in charge of informing the group about the emergency plan.
   c. She wants to tell them how the office floor has been organized.

2. Why do some floors use different staircases than others in the event of an emergency?
   a. because one staircase does not have the capacity to handle all the workers in the building
   b. because the staircases have been designed to prevent some floors from accessing them
   c. because one set of staircases is narrower than the other and is thus deemed unsafe by management

3. What should employees do in case of extreme weather?
   a. They should exit the building by using the appropriate staircase.
   b. They should find a windowless room and huddle together.
   c. They should hide under a desk or table away from glass.

4. What can be inferred about the woman?
   a. She has been hired as the full-time safety inspector for the office building.
   b. She works for the local fire department and visits several offices in a day.
   c. The woman is in charge of giving safety instructions to the workers on her floor.

B **Listen again and choose True or False.**

1. In case of a fire, the listeners should move toward the west exit. [True / False]
2. If everyone in the building used the same staircase, it would slow down the evacuation of the building. [True / False]
3. The elevators in the building are programmed to stop functioning in case of an emergency. [True / False]
4. In extreme weather, workers are asked to protect their heads from flying objects by hiding under desks and tables. [True / False]

Fire Drill

A **Imagine there is a fire drill at your school, and you are in charge of helping students exit the building safely. Complete the instructions with the appropriate information.**

Fire Drill Instructions

Things to do
Things not to do
Where to go
How to get there

B **Now use the notes in the table to say what students should do in the event of a fire.**

Stand up and stay calm. Don't panic. Follow the exit signs and go down the stairs. Walk quickly.

Survivor's Guilt

Reading

A Read the interview. 08-07

The Chicago Reader

August 24th, 2018

Survivor's Guilt

Writer Sunhee Kim

Those who have survived traumatic events where others were injured, sometimes fatally, often experience survivor's guilt. I spoke to Chicago native, Jenna Westman, about her experience with survivor's guilt.

JW The incident happened on the way to our high school senior prom. My boyfriend, Chris, was driving, our friends Kelly and Max were sitting in the backseats, and I was in the passenger's seat. Suddenly, a deer ran across the freeway. Chris slammed on the brakes, but we hit the deer anyway while going about 100 kilometers per hour.

SK What happened next?

JW The deer shattered the windshield. Chris and I had a lot of cuts on our faces and arms, but we were otherwise okay because we were wearing our seatbelts. Kelly and Max, on the other hand, were not okay because they weren't wearing their seatbelts.

SK Oh my goodness.

JW Max died instantly. Kelly's legs and ribs were broken, and she had a punctured lung. She almost died. The EMTs arrived at the scene within five minutes, and because of their fast response, Kelly is alive today. After the accident, I got really depressed. I kept asking myself why I was okay. I would sleep for fourteen or fifteen hours a day. My parents got worried and took me to see a psychologist.

SK Is that where you first heard the term survivor's guilt?

JW Yes, that's right. Survivor's guilt is a form of post-traumatic stress disorder, or PTSD.

SK How did you overcome your depression?

JW Through a lot of therapy and help from family and friends, I was able to come out of my depression.

Comprehension Check Answer the questions about the interview.

1. What is survivor's guilt?
2. Why were Jenna and her friends out that night?
3. Where were Chris, Jenna, Kelly, and Max sitting in the car before the accident?
4. What injuries did Chris and Jenna sustain?

B Do you think you have experienced PTSD in your life?

Writing

Write an essay about why you think it might be difficult to be the only survivor of a large-scale tragedy.

Presentation

A Imagine you have survived a car, train, or plane crash. Complete the table with information about your story of survival.

- **When and where did it occur (year & country, city, ocean, etc.)?**
- **How did you survive?**
- **How (if possible) could the accident have been prevented?**
- **How did the accident change your life?**

B Make a group of five or six students. Then tell your group members about your fictional experience surviving the accident.

In 2002, I survived a snowstorm in Canada. I was driving through the province of Manitoba when a blizzard hit the area. There was lots of snow. The driving conditions were so bad that I had to pull over to the side of the road. Luckily, I was prepared for a situation like this. I had extra blankets, water, and hot packs in my car. I turned off the car engine so I wouldn't use up all of my gasoline. I wrapped myself in the blankets and used the hot packs to keep my hands and face warm. About eight hours later, the storm cleared up, and trucks with snowplows cleared the roads. If I hadn't been prepared, I might not have survived that freezing night.

Wrap-up

A Complete the sentences with the correct words from the word box.

concussion choking electrocuted
emergency room shallow breathing stroke

1. The football player hit his head very hard and suffered a ______________.
2. ______________ is an early sign of a heart attack.
3. Don't let the cat play with that cord! It could get ______________.
4. Jack sprained his ankle badly while playing basketball, so his father took him to the ______________.
5. When feeding grapes to young children, the grapes should be cut in half to prevent ______________.
6. My grandfather suffered a ______________ last year, so now one side of his body is paralyzed.

B Put the sentences in the correct order.

1. you to donate / We need / food and clothes / to the shelter.
2. encouraged me / I could get / to study hard / at my university, so / a good job. / My father
3. will never / My sister / skydiving. / persuade me / to go
4. to help / want me / for a job? / Do you / you look
5. got Andy / believe you / I can't / to fly in / for Dad's / birthday.

C In groups of three or four students, look at the common accidents and think of some ways they can be prevented.

Drivers should put their phones away while driving. Texting and driving causes so many preventable accidents.

D What is the most important thing to remember in an emergency?

Unit 9 Extinction and Endangered Animals

Warm-up

Can you name any of the animals in the pictures? Check the ones you think still exist in the wild today.

1.  ☐

2.  ☐

3.  ☐

4.  ☐

5.  ☐

6.  ☐

7.  ☐

8.  ☐

The Tasmanian Tiger

Conversation

Listen and practice the conversation. 09-01

A Katrina, have you seen the movie *The Hunter*?

B No. What's it about?

A It's about an American hunter who is hired by a corporation to capture the last surviving Tasmanian tiger in Australia.

B I didn't know Australia had large cats.

A The Tasmanian tiger was a carnivorous marsupial, but it was called the Tasmanian tiger because of the distinct dark stripes on its back.

B So what happened in the movie?

A I don't want to spoil it for you, so I'll let you see it for yourself.

B Okay.

A The disturbing thing is that there is film footage of an actual Tasmanian tiger on the Internet. The footage is from 1933.

B Wow, it really makes you realize how recently some animals have gone extinct.

Vocabulary

Fill in the blanks with the letters of the correct pictures.

1. extinction: ______
2. endangered species: ______
3. climate change: ______
4. conservation: ______
5. ozone layer: ______
6. polar ice caps: ______

a.

b.

c.

d.

e.

f.

Listening

A Listen to the conversation and answer the questions. 09-02

1. Why are scientists bringing mammoths back and not another extinct animal?
   a. Mammoths are more interesting.
   b. Mammoths might save us from global warming.
   c. Mammoths can save the Siberian countryside.

2. What is true about the melting polar ice caps?
   a. Warmer weather will be good for the mammoths.
   b. The ice is not melting as fast as scientists thought it was.
   c. Dangerous gases will begin to leak when the ground melts.
3. What can be inferred about the talk?
   a. The woman is surprised by the idea.
   b. The woman will volunteer to fight global warming.
   c. The man will do more research about this topic.

B Listen again and choose True or False.

1. The baby mammoths will be brought up by scientists. [True / False]
2. One problem is that the mammoth is a dangerous predator. [True / False]
3. Mammoths will allow the dirt beneath the earth's surface to get warmer. [True / False]
4. If methane is released into the atmosphere, it will greatly contribute to the climate crisis. [True / False]

TIPS & TIPS crazy

That sounds crazy! / That's crazy! = You can say this to someone who has just told you something amazing, astonishing, or unbelievable.
You drive me crazy! = You can say this to a person who bothers or annoys you.
I'm crazy about ~! = You can say this about something you really like.
***I'm crazy about** Katie Perry's new album!*

Ranking | Reasons Animals Become Endangered or Extinct

Look at the list of reasons animals become extinct or endangered. Do some online research about extinct and endangered animals and then rank them from 1 to 6 with 1 being the most serious threat and 6 being the least serious threat. You may write your own reason in the other space.

climate change ☐	deforestation ☐	disease ☐
loss of habitat ☐	overhunting / poaching ☐	other ☐

Why don't we make a donation?

Conversation

Listen and practice the conversation. 09-03

A I just watched this really upsetting documentary about endangered species.

B Is it the one from the Wildlife Channel?

A Yeah, that's right. The part about the Asian rhinos was just gut-wrenching.

B How many are there left in the wild now?

A About 3,500.

B But those numbers have been increasing, haven't they?

A Local governments have made some progress to stop poaching, but it's still a problem.

B What can we do?

A They need money to hire more people to protect the animals from poachers.

B Why don't we make a donation to a group that funds the effort?

A Okay. How about the Save the Rhino Organization? Its website came up at the end of the documentary.

Pair Work

Choose one of the extinct animals and read the information about the animal. Be sure to choose a different animal than your partner. Then answer the questions below by sharing the information you learned about the animal with your partner.

The **Pinta Island tortoise** was a species of the Galapagos tortoise found on the island of Pinta in the Galapagos Islands group. The Pinta Island tortoise was virtually extinct by the middle of the 19th century because of hunting. Efforts to preserve the creature at that time were not considered, and within a hundred years, the tortoise was thought to be entirely gone. Although scientists believed the Pinto Island tortoise to be extinct, a lone survivor, aptly named Lonesome George, was discovered. Efforts were made to protect George, and attempts were made to mate George with a compatible female in order to produce offspring and to allow the species to survive. Unfortunately, George's mate never produced any viable eggs. Lonesome George died on June 24th, 2012 and he remains a stark reminder of how delicate our planet and its wildlife can be if we are not thoughtful enough to protect it.

The **West African black rhinoceros** lived in the southeastern region of the African continent. In the early 1900s, it suffered a decline in its population due to overhunting although efforts were made in the 1930s to conserve the species. Its numbers increased due to this effort. However, over the following decades, protection of the animal became more relaxed, and its numbers began to decline again. In 2001, there were just five West African black rhinos left in the wild. During the preceding decades, their numbers had been devastated by trophy-hunting, poaching, and killing by farmers trying to protect their crops. Eventually, no trace of the West African black rhinoceros could be found on the African continent, leaving scientists to determine the species had gone extinct. Conservationists believe that more funding and concern for the species could have prevented its extinction.

- Where did the animal live?
- When and why did it become endangered?
- What did conservationists do to protect it?
- When was it finally classified as extinct?

Listening

A Listen to the lecture and change the false statements into true statements. 09-04

1. The passenger pigeon was the most abundant species of bird in South America.
2. Martha lived to be 19 years old and laid two fertile eggs.
3. Passenger pigeons traveled in small flocks.
4. The passenger pigeon was very difficult to hunt.
5. Scientists may attempt to bring the passenger pigeon back by using live DNA tissue.

B Listen again and fill in the blanks.

Ectopistes Migratorius

= 1. ______

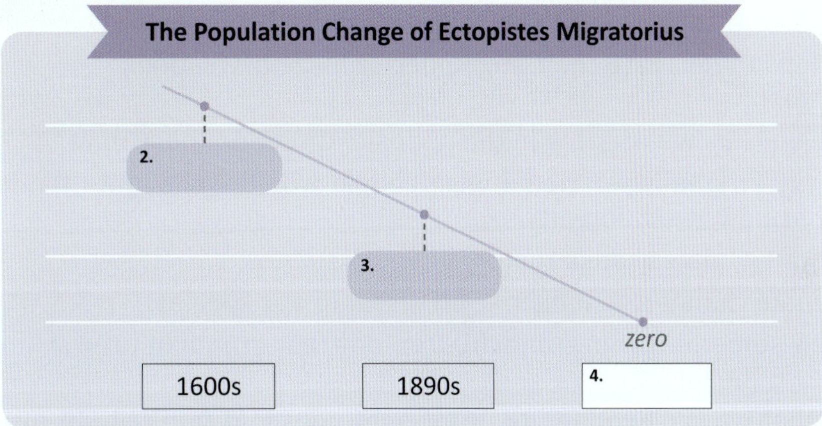

Speaking | An Extinct Animal I'd Like to Bring Back

If you had the power to bring an animal back from extinction, which one would you choose? Find information about an extinct animal and answer the questions. Then share the information with your partner.

1. Extinct Animal Species
2. Time Period When It Lived
3. Size / Appearance / Lifespan
4. When and why did it go extinct?
5. Why do you want to bring this particular animal back?
6. What would the benefits be for the world if it were to return?
7. Are there any downsides to bringing this species back?

I want to bring the dodo back. It disappeared in the late 1600s. It was about one meter tall and weighed between ten and seventeen kilograms. Sailors overhunted the bird, which contributed to its extinction. I really want to see this bird in real life. Its interesting beak and large size really interest me. There are only human drawings of dodos, but I want to see a photograph of one. The downside to bringing it back is that I'm not sure it would really improve society. It would just be neat to look at.

The Human Threat

Conversation

Listen and practice the conversation. 09-05

A What do you think the bigger threat to humanity is, Jin, nuclear war or climate change?

B That's a pretty dark question, Mila. What made you bring that up?

A I've been following the news a lot lately.

B They both concern me to be honest. What do you think?

A In the near future, I'm really concerned about nuclear war. I'd like nations to decrease their stockpiles of nuclear weapons even further.

B But it seems like we're going in the opposite direction these days.

A That's why I'm really worried. I wish people would wake up to the fact that nuclear war could actually bring down humanity.

B What about climate change then?

A I see climate change as a longer-term threat to our species.

B Right. It's something our grandchildren or great-grandchildren will have to deal with at some point down the line.

A It's sad that we can't cooperate more right now, and think about future generations instead of ourselves.

B I wholeheartedly agree!

Grammar

A Let's learn about some time adverbs and adverbial phrases.

lately	right now	these days	in the near future	down the line

Anna and Chen have been doing a lot of volunteer work **lately**.
If we don't leave **right now**, we're going to be late!
Karl is really into judo **these days**. He took a year off from training, but now he's at the gym five days a week.
What kind of technology do you think we will see **in the near future**?
Jaime doesn't see herself getting married anytime soon. It's something she might consider **down the line**.

B Write true sentences about yourself by using the adverbs and adverbial phrases above.

1. ______________________
2. ______________________
3. ______________________
4. ______________________
5. ______________________

Listening

A Listen to the talk and answer the questions. 09-06

1. What is true about infectious diseases in wealthy countries?
   a. They continue to linger in these countries.
   b. They have been mostly eliminated from these countries.
   c. They are in danger of returning to these countries.

2. What happens to children with the measles in some instances?
   a. They can experience nerve damage.
   b. They can experience weakened immune systems.
   c. They can experience cold-like symptoms.

3. What are the symptoms of rubella in adults?
   a. The symptoms are brain swelling and death.
   b. The symptoms might include deafness and blindness.
   c. The symptoms might include a fever and some discomfort.

4. What can be inferred about these infectious diseases?
   a. These diseases are preventable through the use of proper vaccinations.
   b. Children from developed countries are incapable of contracting these diseases.
   c. These diseases were once a problem but are no longer a threat in the world.

B Listen again and fill in the blanks.

Measles	The measles is a disease that can cause 1.__________, diarrhea, breathing problems, and 2.______ swelling. The measles can weaken the 3.________________ of the children.
Rubella	Rubella is a virus that in adults can cause a 4.______ to form all over the body. A fetus that has contracted rubella and survives may experience 5.__________, blindness, or brain 6.__________.

Survey | Vaccinations

Raise your hand if you agree with the statements being read aloud by your teacher. Write the number of students who raised their hands in the blanks to find out which items are agreed upon the most and the least.

	How many
1. Vaccinations should be given to every child in your country.	
2. Parents should have the right not to vaccinate their child.	
3. There are negative effects to receiving vaccinations.	
4. Standard vaccinations should be given to young children in your country.	
5. Vaccinations should be free for children in your country.	
6. Children who do not receive vaccinations should not be allowed to go to school with vaccinated children.	
7. Vaccinations save hundreds of millions of lives every year.	

How Did the Dinosaurs Go Extinct?

Reading

A Read the two emails. 09-07

E-Mail Message

To: jrjacobs@umn.edu
From: sam_44@happymail.com
Date: Sept. 4
Subject: a quick question

Dear Dr. Jacobs,

Thank you so much for your interesting lecture today. The debate surrounding the extinction of the dinosaurs has piqued my curiosity ever since I was a child. During your lecture today, you pointed to two disastrous events, both occurring approximately 65 million years ago, as most likely being responsible for the extinction of the dinosaurs. First, you talked about an asteroid impact in Mexico that would have sent thick clouds of dust into the sky and resulted in the deaths of all living animals and plant life. Second, you mentioned the possibility that massive volcanic eruptions were to blame for the demise of the dinosaurs. I wonder if you lean more strongly toward one theory or the other. I'm very curious because this subject has fascinated me for a large portion of my life, so I'd really appreciate your input.

Sincerely,
Sam Robinson

send

E-Mail Message

To: sam_44@happymail.com
From: jrjacobs@umn.edu
Date: Sept. 5
Subject: RE] a quick question

Dear Sam,

Thank you for your thoughtful email. It's always great to hear from an enthusiastic student. To answer your question, yes, there is one direction I tend to lean toward more strongly than the other. I believe that the asteroid impact theory is weaker than the volcanic eruptions theory. Asteroid impact theorists believe that a meterorite crashed into Mexico's Yucatan Peninsula and vaporized about 65 million years ago. They think this crash spread a layer of the metal iridium across the Earth. They believe this because the iridium that they discovered beneath the Earth's surface dates back to approximately the same time they believe the meteorite crashed into the Earth. The amount of iridium they discovered beneath the Earth's surface also matched the amount an average meteorite would have contained. But I disagree with this theory. You see, the Earth's core consists of magma, and magma also contains large quantities of the metal iridium. I think it's more likely that 65 million years ago, a series of large volcanic eruptions wiped out the dinosaurs. In India, there is evidence of such large volcanic eruptions. These volcanic eruptions, in my opinion, are responsible for the iridium deposits that the scientists have discovered. Of course some scientists disagree with me, and that's what makes scientific inquiry so interesting. We don't always have to agree. We must look at the evidence and make the most informed decision we can.

Yours truly,
Dr. Jacobs

send

Comprehension Check Answer the questions about the emails.

1. What two theories did the professor present to the class in his lecture?
2. Why did Sam Robinson send the email to his professor?
3. What two reasons do scientists give for supporting the asteroid impact theory?
4. What does Professor Jacobs think happened to the dinosaurs?
5. What can be inferred about Professor Jacob's ideas regarding science?

B Based on what you learned in school, why do you think the dinosaurs went extinct?

Presentation

A Go online and look at a list of endangered species. Choose one animal from the list and write an essay about that endangered animal. Include in your essay information such as the animal's habitat, the reasons it became endangered, its current population, and some things we can do to protect it.

B Now make a presentation about your animal.

The Javan rhino is considered critically extinct. Conservationists think there are only 67 left in the wild. The World Wildlife Organization believes there are two things we can do to save the Javan rhino. First, we need to improve its current habitat to make it more comfortable for breeding. Second, we need to start a new population in a different area that would allow a new group to flourish. The WWF needs 5 million dollars to accomplish its goal.

Wrap-up

A Complete the sentences with the correct words from the word box.

extinction　endangered species　climate change　conservation　ozone layer　polar ice caps

1. The African elephant is on the ______________ list.
2. The ______________ of rainforests is important for our planet's future.
3. Now that the ______________ are melting, coastal cities need to worry about their futures.
4. Animal ______________ is a sad reality due to a loss of habitat from ______________.
5. The depletion of the ______________ means we need to be more careful about protecting our skin from the sun.

B Complete the sentences with the correct expressions: *lately, right now, these days, in the near future,* and *down the line*.

1. Michael wants to work for a few years before he goes back to school. But he will definitely go to graduate school at some point ______________.
2. You should put down whatever you're doing ______________ and look at this beautiful sunset. It's stunning!
3. The couple is eating healthier ______________. They've lost a combined ten kilograms.
4. What have you been up to, Marta? I haven't seen you around much ______________.
5. Rob and Sandy are sick and tired of cold winters. I wouldn't be surprised if they moved to a warmer climate ______________.

C Discuss the questions with a partner.

- Do you think human beings will one day end up on the endangered species list?
- Do you think there is enough public awareness about endangered animals?
- Do you think governments are capable of protecting endangered animals?
- Do you think zoos are good places to preserve endangered animals?
- Would you consider volunteering for an organization that protects endangered animals?

D Are there any endangered animals in your country? How about your continent? What can you do to protect endangered animals?

Unit
10 Taking Risks

Warm-up

A Match the kinds of risks with the appropriate pictures. Write PhR for physical risk, ER for emotional risk, and PR for professional risk.

1.

2.

3.

4.

5.

6.

B Which kind of risk are you most likely to take? Why are you most likely to take that kind of risk?

Facing Your Fears

Conversation

Listen and practice the conversation. 10-01

A Stan, you'll never believe what I did this weekend.
B Tell me, Kumiko!
A I went skydiving.
B How is that possible? You're afraid of heights.
A Well, I called a few skydiving companies to ask them if they had any advice for someone in my situation.
B What did they say?
A They said I could do a tandem jump.
B What's a tandem jump?
A A tandem jump is where I'm attached to an instructor and he's the one who pulls the ripcord. All I have to do is hang on.
B Was it scary when you were up there looking down?
A Was it ever. My instructor counted down from three, and that was it. We were free-falling. And I've got to tell you that it was exhilarating!

Group Work **Talk about a fear that you have faced and one that you haven't faced yet but would really like to overcome.**

I used to be afraid of public speaking. The first speech I gave was really tough. I felt nervous the entire time. Over the years, though, my nervousness went away. I'm also afraid of heights. My sister wants to take me bungee jumping, but I'm not sure I can do it. If I could just do it once, I'm sure I could overcome my fear.

Listening

A Listen to a segment of the podcast and answer the questions. 10-02

1. What is Suyoung Park famous for in her country?
   a. She's the youngest female to attempt to summit Mt. Everest.
   b. She's the youngest mountain climber in her country.
   c. She's the youngest person in her country to reach the top of Mt. Everest.

2. How was she introduced to mountain climbing?
   a. Her mother introduced her to members of a climbing club.
   b. Her father enjoys the sport, so he got her into it.
   c. She discovered the joy of climbing in a high school club.

3. What can be inferred about Bob Lemke's podcast?
   a. He often interviews people who have extreme hobbies.
   b. He usually interviews young people who have accomplished a lot.
   c. His podcast is also broadcast on Korean radio.

4. Which of the following statements is correct?
   a. Suyoung Park has climbed mountains on four different continents.
   b. Suyoung Park hopes to climb Mt. Denali before her 18th birthday.
   c. Suyoung Park and her father have plans to climb Mt. Everest again.

B Listen again and choose True or False.

1. Suyoung and her father have wanted to summit Everest for months. [True / False]
2. Suyoung often climbs mountains with her friends. [True / False]
3. Suyoung's father bought her mother a new home appliance. [True / False]

Pair Work

A Ask your partner the questions. Then write your partner's answers in the table.

1.	Would you consider yourself a risk-taker?	□ yes □ no
2.	What's the biggest risk you have taken in your life?	
3.	What was the result of taking the biggest risk?	
4.	Do you partake in any risky habits such as smoking?	
5.	Do you play sports or have hobbies that include taking risks?	
6.	Do you think risk-taking is a negative thing? Should people take risks? If so, how big should the risks be?	

B Find another pair and change partners. Then give a short presentation about your previous partner by using the information in the table.

Jin is a risk-taker. The biggest risk he has taken in his life is going to Australia for a working holiday. While working there, he met a woman from his country. They got married two years later. Jin is a smoker, but he wants to quit. He goes hang gliding on the weekends. It's really dangerous, but he enjoys it. He thinks taking risks is a great thing. He believes that the bigger the risk is, the bigger the reward will be.

I finally quit.

Conversation

Listen and practice the conversation. 10-03

A I did it, Marvin. I put in my two weeks' notice.

B So you're going to sell your soap products full time then? Have you saved enough to quit your full-time job?

A I have $50,000 in savings, but I need $100,000 to really get my startup off the ground.

B How are you going to get the other fifty thousand?

A I went to First National Bank yesterday, and they agreed to give me a loan for $50,000.

B That's great! My wife loves your products. Don't you make them in your house though?

A Not any more. I rented a space and hired a couple college students. I'm in the process of teaching them the manufacturing process. If I'm going to do this full time, then I need to sell larger quantities.

B Have you lined up any supermarkets or grocery stores to sell your products?

A Yes, I have both Grabowski's grocery store and the supermarket chain Z-Mart lined up.

Crossword Puzzle

Read the definitions, find the correct words in the conversation, and complete the puzzle.

Down

1 money borrowed by a person or bank

2 a group of businesses, usually with the same name, that serve the same function and are usually owned by the same company

3 in spite of

4 the food or products sold by a store

Across

5 a new business

6 producing or making something

7 agreeing to pay someone to work at a company or business

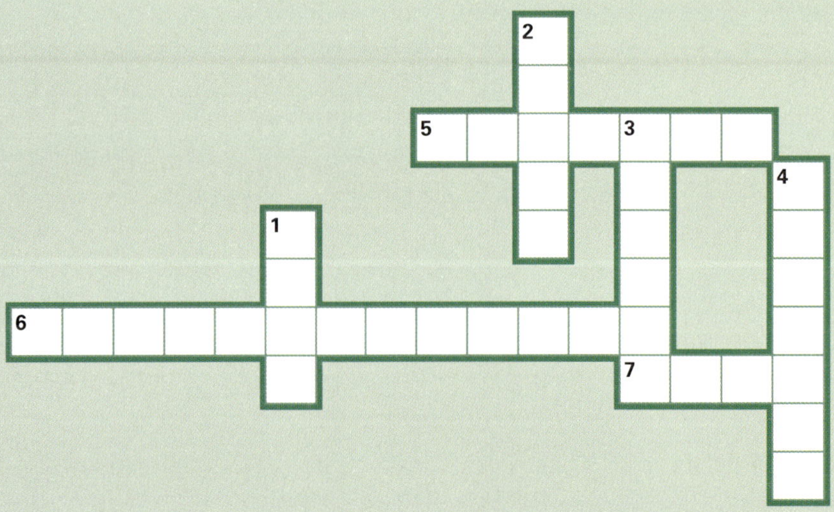

Listening

A Listen to the talk and answer the questions. 10-04

1. Which of the following is NOT mentioned in the talk?
   a. Ask yourself if the market is saturated.
   b. Make sure you hire good employees.
   c. Create a budget for your business.
2. Why does Bernadette advise entrepreneurs to put half of their own money into a venture?
   a. because funding it 100% is too risky
   b. because you need to have some skin in the game
   c. because it shows your employees who the boss is
3. What does Bernadette mention can happen if you borrow money from friends and family?
   a. The relationships will become stronger due to the success of the business.
   b. The business will pull you away from friends and family.
   c. If the business fails, the relationships with those you borrowed from will become strained.
4. Which one of the following questions is NOT mentioned in the talk?
   a. Is it beneficial?
   b. Is it affordable to manufacture?
   c. Is it attractive?

B What are Bernadette's three pieces of advice?

Rating

Rate the following situations from:
1 = There is no way I would do that! to *5* = Yes, I would take that risk!

1.	Skydiving / bungee jumping	
2.	Giving a five-minute speech in front of the class without preparation	
3.	Saying I love you to a partner after the third date	
4.	Quitting a job you hate in order to follow your dream	
5.	Smoking cigarettes / drinking alcohol	
6.	Singing in front of one hundred people	
7.	Performing in a school play or musical	
8.	Learning to drive a car	
9.	Taking a taekwondo class or some other martial arts class	
10.	Learning to fly an airplane or helicopter	
11.	Going whitewater rafting on a river	

Total: ____ / 55

11 – 21 = You like to play it safe. 22 – 33 = You're coming out of your shell.
34 – 44 = You're a tough cookie. 45 – 55 = You're a champ!

Is your father feeling better?

Conversation

Listen and practice the conversation. 10-05

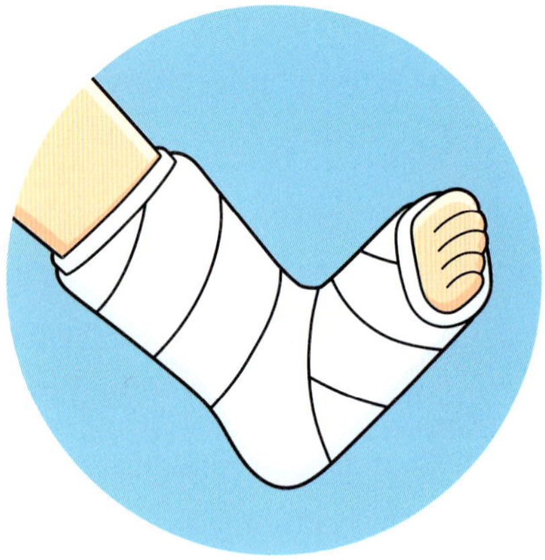

A I heard your father broke his leg.
B Yeah, that's right.
A Is he feeling better?
B Yeah, he's resting at home now. But it was pretty bad.
A What happened?
B He had an accident at work. He's a logger.
A That's a really dangerous job.
B It's the most dangerous job there is. He was cutting down some branches in a tree when he fell.
A How far did he fall?
B About ten meters.
A Oh, my! It could have been much worse.
B That's what my mom said. She wants him to take an office job at the company once he's better.

TIPS & TIPS "I heard (that)..."

I heard that *you got a promotion at work. Congratulations!*
I heard *the city is building a new library this summer.*
My brother heard that *his company might be moving its main office to Austin, Texas.*

Grammar

A Let's learn about past modals.

modal + perfect infinitive (have + past participle)
I **could have won** the race if I had trained harder. Yuki **should have joined** the English club this year. It's really fun. **Would** you **have been** upset if your ex-boyfriend had attended the party? Shaun **must** not **have been** very happy with the traffic this morning. The snow slowed everything down.

B Complete the sentences with the correct forms of the past modals.

1. Annabelle ________________ to the concert. Her favorite band was playing. (should / come)
2. My father ________________ us tonight, but he wasn't feeling well. (would / join)
3. ________ you __________ more comfortable in that chair? It looks like your back is sore now. (wouldn't / be)
4. They ________________ bored at the conference. I heard it was really dull. (must / be)
5. The teacher ________________ more loudly during the lecture. It was very hard to hear her. (could / speak)

Listening

Listen to the two talks and choose the correct answers. 10-06

1-4

1. What happened to Wendy two years ago?
   a. She accepted a job at a university.
   b. She was offered a well-paying job.
   c. She took out a loan for $50,000.
2. What is NOT true about Wendy's situation?
   a. She has to pay back a lot of money she borrowed for school.
   b. She has a good job lined up at a prestigious high school in New York.
   c. She is mad at herself for making a bad decision several years ago.
3. Wendy's dream was to teach high school students in New York City. [True / False]
4. Wendy had a terrible time at graduate school at NYU. [True / False]

5-8

5. What is true about Chao?
   a. He is a college graduate.
   b. He does not have a college diploma.
   c. He plans to graduate from high school soon.
6. Who has access to the Virtual Boardroom?
   a. employees who work for software companies and app developers
   b. workers at corporations who buy the VRB software and glasses
   c. anyone who has virtual reality glasses and an Xbox
7. Chao's company is worth tens of millions of dollars. [True / False]
8. Chao's company was very profitable from the beginning. [True / False]

Group Work Imagine you are going to quit your job in order to start a company. Complete the information in the table and then tell your group about your startup.

Product Your Company Sells or Service Your Company Provides:

____

Company Name:
Office Location:
Your Yearly Salary as CEO:
Benefits (car, stock options, etc.):

Michaela's Jujitsu School

Reading

Read the blog entry. 10-07

www.blogspace.com/blog_michaelasblog

Michaela's Blog

Big News!

Hey there, jujitsu fans! I have some really big news I'd like to share with you. As you know, I've been traveling around North America to compete in jujitsu tournaments for the past ten years. However, I've never been able to quit my job and pursue a professional jujitsu career full time. Now that I'm 30 years old, I know that that dream has passed. I've had a fair bit of success at the competitive level and have thoroughly enjoyed my time there. I've grown a lot over the past ten years. Coming in second place in the black belt division at the Midwestern Classics Tournament last year was the second greatest honor in my life behind receiving my black belt from Master Cesar De Silva. But now it's time to give up competition to focus on a different dream. I've decided to open up my own jujitsu academy right here in Minneapolis, Minnesota. I know I'm taking a big risk by quitting my office job, but I really feel like I'm making the right decision. I've already put down a deposit on a great location although the monthly rent is quite steep. Outfitting the gym with floor mats and other equipment will also be very expensive, but there's something so exciting about running your own school. I thought I would be a lot more nervous than I am. Something in me tells me this dream is going to work out well. I know I'm going to have to put a lot of blood, sweat, and tears into this school in order to make it work, but I've never been afraid of a little hard work. I'll be teaching six classes per day with another two hours during the day available for private lessons. In order for my business venture to work, I need students! If you or anyone you know who lives in the Twin Cities is interested in learning jujitsu, call me at 612-339-9430. I'm glad I have this blog, so I can express my feelings in a public forum like this and tell all of you about my school! If you have any advice for me, please leave it on my comments page. Wish me luck!

Comprehension Check Answer the questions about the blog entry.

1. When did Michaela start competing in jujitsu competitions?
2. How was Michaela's competitive jujitsu career?
3. What was the greatest honor in Michaela's life?
4. What is Michaela's new dream?
5. What does Michaela need in order for her school to be successful?

My 3-Step Plan for My Biggest Dream

A Imagine you have decided to take a big risk by chasing your biggest dream. Make an outline of a 3-step plan that will help you achieve it.

My Dream: ______________________

Step 1: ______________________ → **Step 2:** ______________________ → **Step 3:** ______________________

B Write an essay describing your dream and the three steps necessary to achieve it.

....

....

....

....

C Make a group of four or five students. Then read your essay to your group members.

My dream is to become a helicopter pilot. First, I will go online and find schools in my area that offer classes that fit my schedule. I'll probably have to take classes on the weekends. Next, I will save money for the lessons. I will stop eating out, and I will work overtime in the evenings. Finally, I will graduate and get my helicopter pilot's license so I can legally fly helicopters in the state. Maybe I will be able to earn some extra money by doing commercial flights on weekends.

Wrap-up

A Complete the sentences with the correct words from the word box.

startups	hire	chains	loan	manufacture	grocery

1. Most __________ don't make money in their first few years.
2. When the economy is good, companies tend to __________ more workers.
3. Car companies don't __________ as many cars here as they used to. In fact, more than 70% of production has moved overseas.
4. The popular supermarket has over one hundred __________ in the country.
5. Could you stop by the __________ store? We need some milk and cereal.
6. Clark decided to take out another student __________, so he could attend graduate school.

B Complete the sentences with the correct forms of the past modals.

1. We __________ to the top of the Eiffel Tower when we were in Paris. (should / go)
2. My sister __________ me a ride to school if her car hadn't stalled. (would / give)
3. Sally's friend Kate __________ the party anyway because she had other plans. (couldn't / attend)
4. This diner __________ recently. Everything looks so new! (must / open)
5. What ________ you __________ to him if you had seen him? (would / say)

C Which kinds of risk are you more likely to take? Choose one and then talk about why.

traveling overseas alone · mountain climbing · public speaking
working abroad · quitting a job to follow your dream · skydiving
bungee jumping · performing in front of a thousand people

I'm most likely to travel overseas alone because I'm not scared to try new things. I'm interested in meeting people from other cultures, and I'm not a picky eater. I'll eat anything!

D What is the biggest risk you have taken in your life? What was the result?

Unit 11 Our Solar System

Warm-up

A Look at the pictures related to space. Then write the letters of the correct comments in the boxes.

1. 

2. 

3. 

4. 

a. Look! It's a shooting star.

b. The space station cost 4.2 billion dollars to build.

c. Spacewalking is quite dangerous. A lot can go wrong.

d. Stargazing is probably my favorite hobby.

B Imagine you are a member of a moon colony. What special skills do you think you could contribute to the colony? Make a list of them and share the list with your classmates.

My Contributions

- *I am good at operating a drone.*
-
-
-
-
-

I am really good at operating my drone. I could remotely operate some of the equipment. That could be really useful.

There are thousands of other planets.

Conversation

Listen and practice the conversation. 11-01

A Look at the night sky, Young. Isn't it beautiful?
B It sure is, Jean.
A You know there are thousands of planets out there, right?
B No, there aren't! There are eight planets.
A That's true for our solar system. But there are other solar systems, and they have planets, too.
B Really? How many are there?
A Scientists have confirmed that over 1,800 planets exist in other solar systems.
B That's quite a few. Do you think any of those planets can sustain life?
A I'm not sure, but I know that scientists are looking for such planets in other solar systems' goldilocks zones.
B What's a goldilocks zone?
A It's the area in a solar system where another Earthlike planet would most likely appear.

Build Up Your Knowledge

Take the space quiz.

1. One _____ Earths can fit inside the sun.
   a. thousand b. million c. billion
2. Space officially begins _____ kilometers above the Earth.
   a. 100 b. 1,000 c. 10,000
3. _____ is the hottest planet.
   a. Mercury b. Venus c. Jupiter
4. The word "astronaut" is Greek for _____.
   a. star finder b. space traveler c. star sailor
5. _____ and Venus are planets without any moons.
   a. Mercury b. Jupiter c. Uranus
6. The highest mountain in the solar system is Olympus Mons, located on the planet _____.
   a. Earth b. Mars c. Neptune
7. Scientists think that Jupiter has _____ moons.
   a. 25 b. 67 c. 99
8. The largest object ever sent to space is the _____.
   a. *International Space Station*
   b. *New Horizons space* probe
   c. *Curiosity* Mars rover

Listening

A Listen to the talk and answer the questions. 11-02

1. What did the IAU do in 2006 that upset a number of people?
   a. It changed the definition of a planet.
   b. It declared Pluto a dwarf star.
   c. It decided on the definition of a moon.
2. Which of the following is NOT part of the IAU's definition of a planet?
   a. A planet must be the dominant object in its orbit.
   b. A planet must orbit the Earth.
   c. A planet must possess a round shape.
3. What was an unexpected result of the IAU's decision to downgrade Pluto?
   a. Scientists were upset because their previous research needed to be changed.
   b. Other planets in our solar system were now in danger of being downgraded.
   c. The IAU underestimated people's personal affection for the planet Pluto.
4. Which state in the U.S. still gives Pluto planetary status?
   a. Texas
   b. Mexico
   c. New Mexico

B Listen again and choose True or False.

1. IAU stands for International Astronomical University. [True / False]
2. The IAU was prepared for the public's response to its announcement. [True / False]
3. Pluto consists mostly of ice and rock. [True / False]
4. In many old textbooks, our solar system is said to have eight planets. [True / False]

Discussion

Make a group of three to four students. Then discuss the questions with your group members.

- What is your favorite planet?
- Have you ever dreamed of traveling to space?
- Do you think humans will vacation on the moon in the near future?
- Should governments continue to invest in space travel? Why or why not?
- How have satellites made your life better? Give specific examples.
- What is your favorite movie set in space?
- Do you believe there is life on other planets?

A What is your favorite planet?
B I like Jupiter because one of its moons, Europa, might be habitable for humans.
C I've always been a huge fan of Mars ever since I saw the movie *Total Recall*.

Another NASA Invention

Conversation

Listen and practice the conversation. 11-03

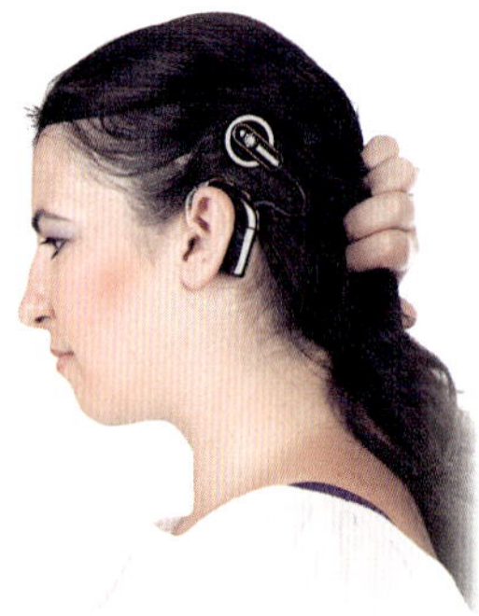

A I saw a really interesting documentary on the Science Channel the other day.

B What was it about?

A It was about NASA. Its engineers have invented so many interesting items.

B Like what?

A Cochlear implants, for example, were invented by a NASA scientist.

B What is a cochlear implant?

A It's a device that allows people with hearing impairments to hear again.

B My cousin is hearing impaired. I think she might use one. What does it look like?

A It has a piece of plastic that wraps behind the ear and a tube that reaches into the ear.

B That's it.

A Adam Kissiah, an engineer at the Kennedy Space Center, developed the technology. He suffered from hearing loss himself and had grown frustrated with traditional hearing aids.

Inventions of NASA

Look at the pictures and guess which ones were invented by NASA engineers.

1.
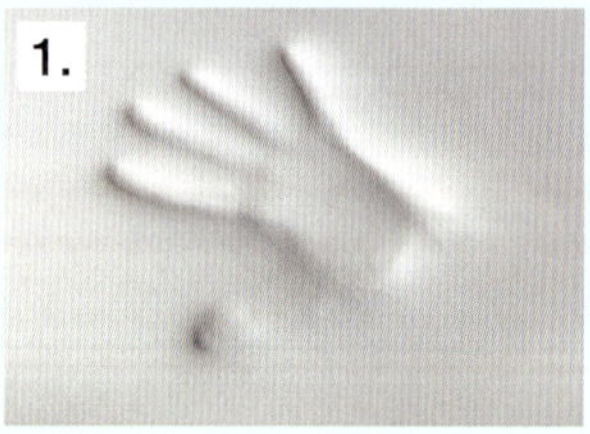
memory foam

2.

powdered drink mix

3.

water filters

4.

solar panels

5.
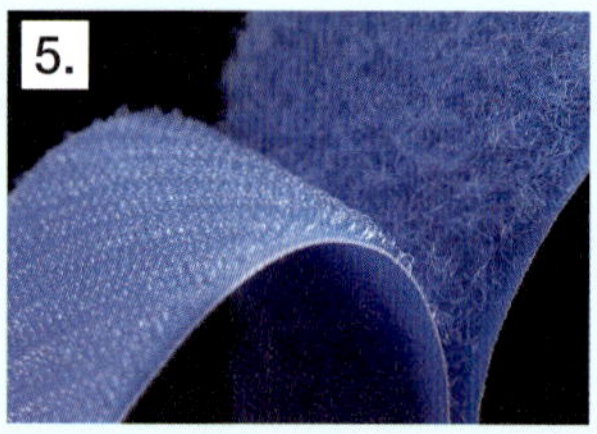
Velcro

6.

smoke detectors

7.

scratch-resistant lenses

8.
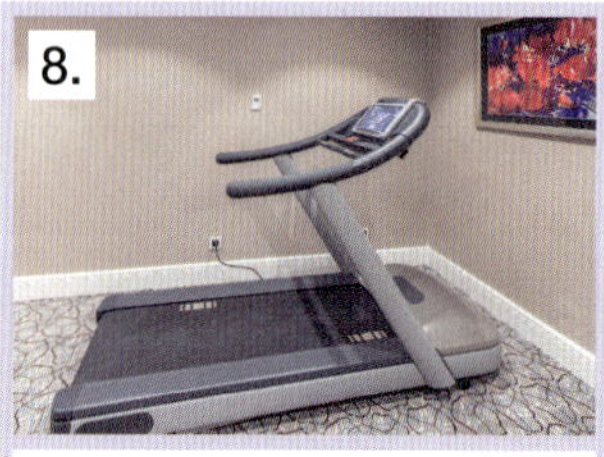
running machine

9.

Teflon

Listening

A Listen to the conversation and answer the questions. 11-04

1. What is Peggy Whitson's rank for the amount of time spacewalking?
   a. She is first.
   b. She is second.
   c. She is third.
2. How much time did Michael Lopez-Alegria spend outside the spacecraft in space?
   a. He spent 82 hours and 22 minutes outside the spacecraft.
   b. He spent 67 hours and 40 minutes outside the spacecraft.
   c. He spent 22 hours and 40 minutes outside the spacecraft.
3. Who has spent the most days in space?
   a. Michael Lopez-Alegria
   b. Valery Polyakov
   c. Sergei Adveyev
4. What happens to astronauts when they have spent long periods of time in space?
   a. Their bodies become stronger in zero gravity.
   b. Their muscles and bones deteriorate in space.
   c. They become tired, and their minds become weaker.

B Listen again and choose True or False.

1. Spacewalking is time spent in space inside a spacecraft. [True / False]
2. Anatoly Solovyev spent more than three days spacewalking. [True / False]
3. Some American astronauts have recorded the most time in space. [True / False]
4. Sergei Adveyev spent more than a year in space without returning to the Earth. [True / False]

Group Work

A Imagine you and your group members are stranded on the surface of the moon. Rank the items in the box from 1 most important to 10 least important. Give reasons for your answers.

	Items	Ranking	Reasons
1.	a first-aid kit		
2.	water		
3.	matches		
4.	military food rations		
5.	a star map		
6.	oxygen tanks		
7.	a heater		
8.	a spacesuit		
9.	a compass		
10.	a pocket knife		

B Now compare some of the items on your list to items on the other groups' lists. Why did you agree or disagree on certain items?

A Manned Mission to Mars

Conversation

Listen and practice the conversation. 11-05

A Have you seen the movie *The Martian*?

B Yes, I have. Do you think humans will ever really go to Mars?

A Absolutely! Do you know who Elon Musk is?

B Yes, I do. He's the maker of the Tesla automobile.

A Exactly. He also founded a company called Space X.

B What does Space X do?

A Its engineers are working on all kinds of projects, but one of the projects is a rocket that will take people from the Earth to Mars.

B Why does he want to send people to Mars?

A His long-term goal is to create a Martian colony. I read he imagines up to a million people will one day live in a Martian colony.

B It's a very inhospitable environment though.

A You've got that right. Engineers will have to work around a lot of obstacles in order to make it happen. Some experts doubt that it's possible.

B They said the same thing about the moon landing.

A That's true.

Useful Expressions

A Let's learn about phrasal verbs using *work*.

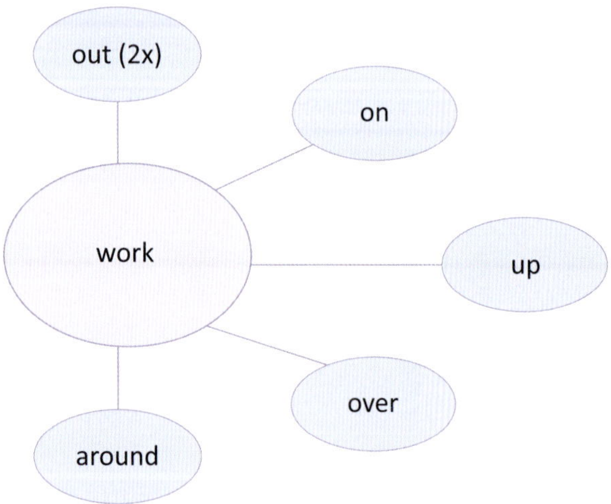

Examples

Pam **works out** every day. She's healthy.

Carol **worked out** the difficult math problem.

Let's **work on** the presentation together.

It is hard to **work up** the courage to ask someone out on a date.

Young had to **work over** his creative writing assignment to come up with a better ending.

The team had to **work around** my busy schedule.

B Fill in the blanks with the correct prepositions.

1. The playwright worked __________ the first act of his play several times before he was satisfied with the draft.
2. Saydee does not like to work __________ her homework on weekends. She would rather play with her friends Christine and Caroline.
3. You should work __________ at least three times a week in order to maintain a healthy body weight.

4. The builders had to work __________ logistical problems like bad weather and heavy street traffic during the day.

5. Engineers at NASA must work __________ very complex math formulas every day.

6. Jin worked __________ the courage to ask Suyoung out on a date. Now they are boyfriend and girlfriend.

Listening

A Listen to the interview and answer the questions. 11-06

1. What is the purpose of the Mars One mission?
   a. Their goal is to colonize Mars with robots.
   b. Their goal is to colonize the planet Mars with humans.
   c. Their goal is to contact lifeforms on Mars.

2. What is true about the colonists on the Mars One mission?
   a. They will return to the Earth after several years.
   b. They will travel to Mars with their spouses.
   c. They will never return to the Earth.

3. How will the colonists survive on Mars?
   a. They will bring the supplies they need with them.
   b. Supplies will be sent prior to the colonists' arrival.
   c. Supplies will be sent once they have arrived.

4. How many years will have passed by the time all twenty colonists are on Mars?
   a. eight years
   b. ten years
   c. twelve years

B Listen again and write the correct words in the blanks.

"We started with over 200,000 1.__________. But by the time we are ready to send people to Mars, it will be 2.__________ down to just twenty."

"The first 3.__________ mission is set to arrive on 4.__________ in 2032."

"We are going to send four 5.__________ on the first mission and four more every two years after that until there are twenty colonists living there."

Group Work

A Make a group of four or five students. Now imagine that life on Earth is going extinct and that the only way to survive is to travel to the Mars colony. However, the Mars colony only has room for three people, which means one or two of your group members must stay behind. Make a case for why you should be allowed to join the Mars colony.

> I think I should go to the Mars colony because I am good at building things. I make furniture in my free time, so I can make useful items on Mars. I can also repair items that have been broken.

B Now vote for the three members of your group who will go to the Mars colony. You cannot vote for yourself.

Going Up?

Reading

A Read the article. 11-07

Science Weekly Magazine

Going Up?

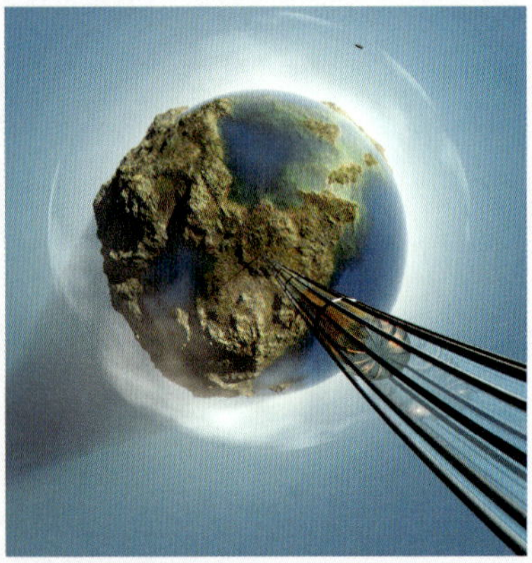

Each week, we try to give readers of *Science Weekly Magazine* information about the latest scientific innovations shaping our lives. But this week I am going to talk about an idea that has been floating around for more than a hundred years but has yet to be built: a space elevator. Although scientists and engineers have been unable to build a functional space elevator as of yet, they are on the cusp of creating one, and it would change the way we travel to space forever. The space elevator is a concept that involves fastening an extraordinarily long cable, 35,786km in length to a point near the Earth's equator to a counterweight beyond the Earth's atmosphere in space. The cable would need to be made of material strong enough and light enough to withstand the Earth's gravitational pull. The top end of the space elevator would act as a counterweight and would be held up by the centrifugal force of the Earth's constant rotation. Once the cable is secured to the Earth and to the counterweight in space, objects and people could be elevated into space or brought back down with relative ease. There would be no more need to use jet propulsion in order to deliver payloads to space. Instead, the space elevator would send payloads to the space station at the top end of the cable. Although this all sounds like science fiction, engineers are currently working on making a cable out of material strong enough to withstand the Earth's gravitational pull. Some of the materials they are experimenting with include carbon nanotubes, baron nitride nanotubes, and diamond nano-threads. What would a world with a space elevator look like? Perhaps we will find out sooner than later.

Comprehension Check Answer the questions about the article.

1. How long has the idea for the space elevator been in existence?
2. In what region of the Earth would the beginning point for the space elevator need to be built?
3. What must be true about the cable on the space elevator in order for it to work?
4. What will hold the counterweight up in space, and stop it from crashing into the Earth?
5. What would the benefit of the space elevator be?

B Do you think the space elevator will one day become a reality?

Presentation

Imagine you could start a Mars colony with three famous or infamous people from the present or the past. Who would you choose and why?

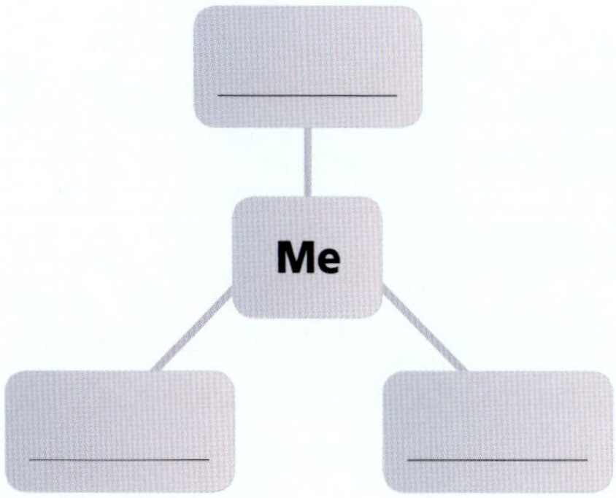

Writing

Would you travel to the Mars colony if it meant you could never return to the Earth or see your family again?

How to Survive on Mars

Human survival is dependent on three key factors: air, water, and food. But how would colonists get these necessary resources on Mars?

Air

Humans require oxygen to live. The Mars Oxygen In Situ Resource Utilization Experiment, or MOXIE, for short, is an experimental machine that will be part of the Mars 2020 rover mission. The machine is designed to pull oxygen out of Mars' thin atmosphere. If the experiment is a success, we will be one step closer to colonizing the planet.

Water

Humans can survive for about three days without water. So where would a colonist on Mars find drinking water? Some scientists suggest loading Martian soil, which contains tiny ice crystals, into a machine that can melt the ice crystals and produce water. Others recommend getting drinkable water from Mars' polar ice caps, where it is plentiful.

Food

In order to grow food on Mars, the colonists would need to come equipped with the proper materials to build a greenhouse. They would also need to choose the right crops. Scientists are now studying which kinds of fruits and vegetables would grow the best on Mars. Since the soil is very thin and lacks nutrients, human waste is one of the materials that could be used to enrich the soil although it doesn't sound very appealing.

Wrap-up

A Use the NASA inventions in the word box to complete the sentences.

running machine	water filter	scratch-resistant lenses
solar panels	memory foam	smoke detector

1. Almost every house in the United States and around the world is equipped with a ____________. It has saved countless lives over the years.
2. Our new mattress was made using a layer of ____________. It's incredibly comfortable and forms to my specific body shape.
3. These sunglasses are terrible! I'm going to buy new ones with ____________. Then, I won't have to be so careful with them.
4. Drinking tap water can be a little dangerous. I recommend using a ____________.
5. My father had ____________ installed on the roof of our house, and it has reduced our monthly energy bills by 80%.
6. I have a ____________ in my basement, but I never use it. I don't have time to exercise these days.

B Fill in the blanks with the correct prepositions: *around, on, out, over,* and *up*.

1. Alice had to work ________ the math problem in her head for a few moments before she could begin writing it out.
2. Seung likes to work ________ in the morning because it gives her energy throughout the day.
3. Chen and his wife are working ________ their house. They're building a deck and installing a swing set for the children.
4. Children need to work ________ their differences without adults always interfering.
5. It took a lot for Michaela to work ________ the courage to jump off the highest diving board at the swimming pool.
6. The construction crew had to work ________ the unpredictable weather that was disrupting the completion of the project.

C Imagine you have been asked to join a crew of astronauts traveling to Europa, one of Jupiter's moons. You will see things most people will never get to see, but you will have to leave your family and friends for twelve years. Take notes of the good points and bad points of accepting this mission.

D Say why you would or would not accept the mission in C. Use the notes to give your answers.

Unit 12 Accomplishments and Celebrations

Warm-up

A Say what you think has just happened in each of the pictures.

B What recent accomplishments are you the proudest of? How did you celebrate them?

He got it!

Conversation

Listen and practice the conversation. 12-01

A Hon, I'm home!
B I'm in the living room!
A Hey!
B I'm glad you're here. I've got some exciting news.
A Me, too! Tell me yours first.
B You know that audition Shane did for the school play?
A Yeah.
B He got it! The director gave him the leading role.
A That's great. I know he worked hard for that part.
B He sure did. He rehearsed for over a month.
A Where is he? I want to congratulate him.
B He's at a bonfire at a cast member's house.
A Oh, I see. We'll have to do something special this weekend to celebrate.
B Why don't we eat out at the Centerville Steakhouse on Saturday evening? By the way, what is your good news?
A I've been promoted to district sales manager.
B Congratulations! We have a lot to celebrate this weekend.

TIPS & TIPS Terms of Endearment

Terms of endearment are to be used by spouses, romantic partners, etc.
***Honey**, I'm home!*
*Hey, **hon**. How was your day?*
*Hello, **darling**!*
*Happy Valentine's Day, **sweetheart**!*
*Good morning, **sweetie**!*

Vocabulary

Write definitions for the following vocabulary. Use a dictionary if necessary.

1. bonfire	
2. graduation ceremony	
3. anniversary party	
4. retirement party	
5. christening	
6. family gathering	
7. parade	
8. barbecue	

Listening

A Listen to the conversation and answer the questions. 12-02

1. What is true about the two speaker's children?
   a. They both attend Penn State.
   b. Their graduation parties are on the same day.
   c. They socialize together.

2. What is the man's plan?
   a. His family will go to his nephew's party instead of Stephanie's graduation party.
   b. His family will attend his nephew's party after he attends the party at Katherine's house.
   c. His family will show up to Stephanie's graduation party after his nephew's party.

3. What can we infer about Stephanie's age?
   a. She's the same age as Steven.
   b. Steven is younger than her.
   c. She's younger than Steven.

4. What can be inferred about Katherine?
   a. She is talking to Mike for the first time.
   b. She has met Mike several times.
   c. She is friends with Mike's wife.

B Listen again and choose True or False.

1. Stephanie's graduation party is on June 22nd. [True / False]
2. Mike's family is unable to attend Stephanie's graduation party. [True / False]
3. Mike's nephew's party begins three hours before Stephanie's. [True / False]
4. Steven wants to attend the same university as Stephanie. [True / False]

Speaking

Imagine it is the year 2090. Tell the story of your life and all of your accomplishments by using the timeline below.

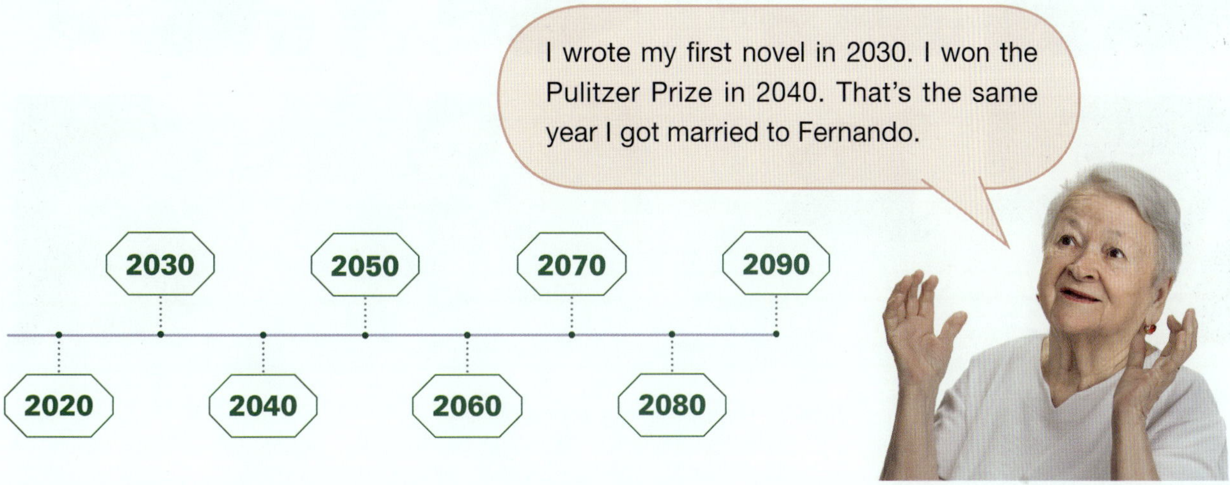

You ran it in under three hours?

Conversation

Listen and practice the conversation. 12-03

A So how did you do in the marathon on Saturday, Mandy?
B Not bad, Bret. My time was 2 hours and 57 minutes.
A You ran it in under three hours?
B Yeah, I'm quite proud of my time actually.
A You should be. My brother-in-law runs marathons all the time, and his average time is around three and a half hours.
B I used to run a lot in college, but that was ten years ago.
A What was your best mile time in college?
B My best mile time was something like 4 minutes and 50 seconds.
A Wow! I don't think I've ever run a mile in under seven minutes in my life.
B That's okay. You're more of a team-sports person. You played basketball, right?
A That's right. But I'd like to run a marathon someday.
B Why don't you start with a 10k and see how you like it?
A Okay. How do I start?
B I'll make a training program for you tonight. I'll give it to you tomorrow.
A Great, thanks!

Speaking

What do you think the people in the pictures have accomplished?

Eric has just been elected to public office. I think he is now the mayor of a big city.

Listening

Listen to two people talking about their accomplishments and choose the correct answers. 12-04

1-4

1. What kind of doctor does Yuki's fiancé want to be?
   a. He wants to be an ER doctor.
   b. He wants to be a general practitioner.
   c. He wants to be a surgeon.
2. What is true about Yuki and her fiancé?
   a. They want to be the same kind of doctor.
   b. They work at the same location.
   c. They own a business together.
3. Yuki's job prevents her from sleeping some nights. [True / False]
4. Yuki wants to get married in her home country. [True / False]

5-8

5. What has been Sumin's dream for a long time?
   a. He has wanted to be a production assistant at the Live Shopping Network.
   b. He has wanted to meet the on-air talent at the Live Shopping Network.
   c. He has wanted to be in front of the camera at the Live Shopping Network.
6. What is NOT true about Sumin's new job?
   a. He will be making more money.
   b. He will be producing his own shows on the network.
   c. He will be working with some of his heroes.
7. Sumin spent five years working as a production assistant at the Live Shopping Network. [True / False]
8. Sumin's roommate submitted a video of Sumin pretending to sell items in their living room. [True / False]

Presentation | My Greatest Accomplishment

Answer the questions about your greatest accomplishment and give a presentation to your group members about it.

1. What is your greatest accomplishment?
2. How did you achieve it?
3. Who, if anyone, helped you achieve it?
4. Why do you think this is your greatest accomplishment?
5. What was the biggest challenge?

My team worked hard on that project.

Conversation

Listen and practice the conversation. 12-05

A Kyung, can I talk to you for a minute?
B Sure, Mr. Lee. What can I do for you?
A I just want to tell you that I'm very happy with the work your team did on the Vanderbilt Residence.
B Thank you.
A Your team completed the project a week early, and you met the budget. The CEO is very pleased.
B My team worked really hard on that project, so they deserve most of the credit.
A The CEO has approved a $1,000 dinner budget as a thank you for your team. I'm giving the money to you, and I'll let you decide the details of the dinner.
B That's very generous, Mr. Lee. Thank you.
A It's our pleasure. There's another project in uptown that I'd like to give to your team. It's a bigger project and is more complicated, but I trust your team is plenty capable.
B We're ready for anything.
A Great. I just need to get the CEO to sign off on it, and it'll be your team's project.
B Fantastic.

Grammar

A Let's learn about causative verbs.

1. let + person + base verb Jack **lets his daughter watch** horror movies. **2. make + person + base verb** The professor **made the students write** two essays last week.	**4. help + person + infinitive (or without *to*)** Ellen **helped Marcus (to) study** for his English test.
3. have + person + base verb / have + thing + past participle I will **have my husband call** your husband with details about the picnic. Soyung **had her prescription refilled** at the local pharmacy.	**5. get + person + infinitive** Johan **gets Sandy to give** him a ride to school every day.

B Fill in the blanks with the correct forms of the causative verbs and main verbs in the box.

let / watch   make / stay   have / look   have / pull   help / pay   get / go

1. Our boss ______ us ______ late on Friday evening, so we missed the bus and had to take a taxi to our house.
2. I don't ______ my son ______ scary movies before bed because he won't be able to sleep.
3. We can't ______ Rick ______ out on weekends. He always wants to stay home and watch television.
4. Her parents always ______ her ______ her bills. I don't think it's healthy.

5. Mai _______ her rotten tooth _______ at the dentist's office yesterday.

6. Can you _______ your father _______ at my car? He's an excellent mechanic.

Listening

A Listen to the conversation and answer the questions. 12-06

1. How does Pearl feel about graduating from university?
   a. She's very excited about it.
   b. She feels happy, but worried.
   c. She is worried about her school debt.

2. Why doesn't Pearl want to attend graduate school?
   a. She thinks it will be too expensive.
   b. She thinks it's going to be too difficult.
   c. She doesn't think her major is useful.

3. What does Dillon plan to do after graduation?
   a. He plans to go to graduate school.
   b. He plans to learn how to write movies.
   c. He plans to become a history professor.

4. What can we infer about the two people?
   a. They once attended the same course.
   b. They both studied the same major.
   c. They are boyfriend and girlfriend.

B Listen again and change the false statements into true statements.

1. Pearl thinks she will work in education after college.

2. Dillon and Pearl are graduating from high school.

3. The Renaissance is Pearl's favorite period in history.

4. Pearl thinks Dillon's short stories were really scary.

Group Work

A In groups of three or four students, ask and answer the questions about your school and career choices.

1. When did/will you graduate from university?
2. How do you feel about your chosen major?
3. Would you like to go to university to study a completely new major? If yes, what major would you like to study?
4. If you could go back to your senior year of high school, what would you change?
5. How would you define the word "successful?"

B Were there any similar answers in your group? If so, what were they?

The Wedding Planner

Reading

Read the interview. 12-07

Wonderful Weddings Magazine

Writer: Erica Stevens

No one on the planet knows weddings like Raphael Martinez, a New York City native and the city's most sought-after wedding planner. I sat down with Raphael at a quaint little coffee shop in Manhattan to discuss his career and to pick his brain for any advice he might be able to give the readers of Wonderful Weddings Magazine.

ES When it comes to wedding celebrations, you're the person to call. How did you get into this business, Raphael?

RM After college, I got a job as an assistant to a very well-known wedding planner named Gabrielle Barnett. I was her assistant for five years before I branched out on my own. She taught me everything I know.

ES What does being a wedding planner entail?

RM A wedding planner must be a great visionary. I imagine the most amazing celebration, and then I try to turn that into a reality. You see, I can't bake a cake, take a good photograph, or arrange flowers, but I'm an excellent coordinator. I can take care of every last detail by putting together the best team of people.

ES So your expertise has more to do with timing and coordination?

RM Exactly. But I'm also a people person. You have to be able to speak your mind. Couples are paying me for my knowledge about weddings, and I know what works and what doesn't work. I'm not afraid to tell the bride and groom the truth.

ES I heard brides can be especially difficult.

RM Oh, yes. But I've been doing this for fifteen years. I know exactly what to say to them to put their minds at ease.

ES Do you have any advice for our readers?

RM Most people can't afford an extravagant wedding, and that's okay. Plan the wedding that you want. A small wedding with only ten very close family members and friends can be more special and memorable than a huge wedding with 1,000 guests.

ES That's great advice. Thank you for talking to us today.

RM You're welcome.

Comprehension Check Answer the questions about the interview.

1. How did Raphael Martinez get into wedding planning?
2. What should a wedding planner be according to Raphael?
3. How does Raphael prefer to communicate with brides and grooms?
4. What advice does he give the readers of *Wonderful Weddings Magazine*?

Group Work

A Write a short essay describing your perfect wedding.

B Make a group of four or five students. Read your essays to your classmates.

My perfect wedding would be really small. It would be outside on a beach in Southern California. Only our immediate family members and best friends would attend. After the wedding ceremony, we would meet at a park for a barbecue and live music. It would be wonderful!

A Wedding Budget

Imagine you have $15,000 to plan a wedding. The bride and groom are allowed to keep any unspent money. Find the information including prices for the following wedding services. Then decide how much you are willing to spend on each service.

		Budget: $15,000
Location (wedding hall, church, etc.)		$________
Food / Drinks		$________
Wedding Presents (rings, watches, etc.)		$________
Dress / Tuxedo		$________
Photos		$________
		Total Price: $________

Wrap-up

A Complete the sentences with the correct words in the word box.

bonfire   graduation ceremony   anniversary party   retirement party   parade   barbecues

1. The Mitchells decided to have a ______________ in the fire pit in their backyard. They invited our family to join them.
2. Andre worked at the same company for thirty years. The company threw him a very nice ____________ when he retired last year.
3. Sarah's parents had an ______________ last week. They've been married for twenty-five years.
4. Every summer, the city of White Bear Lake hosts the Manitou Day ______________. The people on the long line of floats throw candy to the bystanders.
5. On the 4th of July, many Americans have ______________ where they grill hot dogs and hamburgers with their families and friends.
6. I took a great picture of my daughter in her cap and gown at her high school ______________.

B Fill in the blanks with the correct forms of the causative verbs and main verbs.

1. Ming _______ her neighbors _______ the leaves in their yards. (help / rake)
2. Jia _______ her daughter _______ her homework after school every day. (make / do)
3. Jane _______ her boyfriend _______ her self-defense. I think that was a good idea. (get / teach)
4. I'll _______ my accountant _______ your firm. (have / contact)
5. My parents _______ their house _______ last summer. (have / paint)
6. I don't _______ my dog _______ around off its leash at the park. (let / run)

C Complete a short survey about your classmates' accomplishments by using the questions in the card. Then use the data from your survey to answer the questions below.

Question 1. What accomplishment are you the proudest of?
Question 2. How did you accomplish it?

1. What was the most common answer to question one?
2. What kinds of answers did you receive for question one?
3. What was the most interesting response to question one?
4. Who do you think worked the hardest to accomplish something?
5. Was there an accomplishment mentioned that you would someday like to achieve? If yes, what is it?

Answer Key

Unit 1

Hopes and Dreams

India was incredible!

Listening p. 13

Script

A: Hey, Millie, how's life in Los Angeles?

B: Not bad, Chang. How are things in Boston?

A: It's so cold here! So where do you live in L.A.?

B: I live in an area called Los Feliz. It's next to Hollywood.

A: Cool. What are you doing for work out there?

B: I want to be an animator, so I'm doing an internship at an animation studio in Culver City.

A: Cool. But aren't internships usually unpaid?

B: That's right. I also work evenings at a coffee shop in my neighborhood to pay some of my bills.

A: Some?

B: My parents are helping me cover the rest. They said they'd help me for one year, and then they'll cut me off.

A: That's fair.

B: I thought so too, but it's been eight months now, so I've only got four months to find a real job in animation that will pay my bills.

A: You were the best artist at our college. If anyone can find a good job in the entertainment industry, it's you. By the way, my uncle works for an animation studio. Why don't I give you his number? Maybe he's hiring.

B: Are you serious? That would be great.

A: No problem. I'll text you his number.

A

1. b 2. a 3. c
4. c 5. b

B

1. False 2. False 3. False
4. True 5. False

I'm dropping out.

Useful Expressions p. 14

B

1. need 2. make
3. think, will 4. made
5. needs 6. thought, had

Listening p. 15

Script

1. I'm Kayla, and my dream was to become a fashion model. When I was a little girl, I used to wear my mother's high heels and walk around the kitchen imagining it was a catwalk. I loved visiting my aunt's house because she had all the best fashion magazines. When I turned 13, I asked my parents to buy me subscriptions to those magazines as birthday and Christmas presents. When I was 16, I won a fashion contest at a local mall. I'm 21 years old now, and I live in New York. I've been a professional fashion model in New York for three years. Next month, I'm going to go to Paris for three months for a big modeling job. It's for a world-famous fashion brand.
2. Hey, I'm Justin, and I'm part of a breakdancing group called X Street. I've been a member of X Street for two years. I joined the group on my fifteenth birthday. X Street is a professional breakdancing group that performs all over the United States and Europe. I got into breakdancing when I was ten. I really love hip-hop music, so it made sense that I would get into breakdancing. I love the acrobatic nature of this kind of dancing. It's really difficult to learn and looks really cool when it's done correctly. My dream is to become a rapper. I love to write and record my own music. When I'm too old to breakdance, I'm going to work behind the scenes in the music business. I'm going to study to become a sound engineer so I can learn how to record my music professionally.

A

1. Kayla wanted magazine subscriptions as birthday and Christmas presents when she was young.
2. Kayla is moving to Paris next month.
3. Justin travels around the world dancing.
4. Justin plans to study sound engineering when he is too old to perform with X Street.

B

	Kayla	Justin
Age	21	17
Dream Job	fashion model	rapper
Current Status	working as a model in New York	professional dancer

The Learning Annex

Vocabulary p. 16

1. f 2. e 3. b
4. a 5. d 6. c
7. h 8. g

Listening p. 17

Script

A: How's your class at the community center going, Stephanie?

B: Oh, it's wonderful, Rolf. I'm learning Chinese. My husband, Ming, wants me to be able to talk to his parents. They only speak Chinese.

A: Wow, that's quite ambitious. I heard Chinese is very difficult to learn.

B: It's actually not that difficult for native English speakers. The English and Chinese languages share a common sentence structure, but saying the words correctly is very difficult. How about you? Are you studying anything at the moment?

A: No. I just finished a class in car maintenance. My wife asked me to take the class so I could fix minor problems with our cars or change the oil in them.

B: Cool. That'll save you some money in the long run. Have you had to fix any car problems yet?

A: Actually, I changed the oil in my wife's car last weekend. It took me longer than it would have if I'd gone to a mechanic, but I saved about $40.

B: That's awesome. I bet your wife was happy.

A: She sure was. She decided to use the money we would have spent on an oil change to go out for dinner.

B: Where did you go?

A: We went to a Chinese restaurant. Maybe next time we can go on a double-date with you and your husband. You can order for the whole table.

B: Sounds good. I'll get to practice my Chinese!

A

1. c	**2.** c	**3.** a
4. c	**5.** b	

B

1. False	**2.** False	**3.** False
4. False	**5.** False	

The Appalachian Trail

Reading p. 18

Comprehension Check

1. She was planning to backpack across Europe.
2. You have to buy airline tickets, and pay for food and hostels.
3. Benton MacKaye conceived the idea.
4. They are going to start in Georgia and finish in Pennsylvania.
5. It's a very long trail, and it's hot in the summer.

Wrap-up p. 20

A

1. thought, had	**2.** made
3. thinks, will	**4.** need
5. make	**6.** need
7. thought, had	

Unit 2 A.I.

Warm-up p. 21

1. d	**2.** c	**3.** e
4. b	**5.** a	**6.** f

Siri, where is the Taj Mahal located?

Vocabulary p. 22

A

1. technophobe
2. virtual reality
3. technophile
4. cyborg
5. robotics
6. artificial intelligence
7. autonomous car
8. computer literate

Listening p. 23

Script

Good morning, class! I'd like to talk to you today about the singularity. The singularity is a term that was coined by the mathematician John von Neumann in 1950. It is the idea that artificial intelligence, or A.I., will one day become so advanced that it will surpass human intelligence. Some scientists believe that in the near future, A.I. will no longer need human programmers in order to upgrade its performance. A.I. will be capable of upgrading itself until it is more intelligent than any human on Earth. It is hotly debated when the singularity will occur, with some experts believing it will happen within ten years and others believing it will happen more toward the end of the century. Regardless of when the singularity occurs, many scientists believe it is inevitable and that human beings should be working on ways to control it. Some scientists predict a dangerous future where the machines have evolved beyond any need for humans and thus want to destroy us. Other scientists imagine a peaceful future where humans exist side by side with machines and machines do most of the work while humans enjoy more leisure time.

A

1. The term "singularity" was coined in 1950.
2. The singularity is the idea that A.I. will one day surpass human intelligence.
3. Some experts agree the singularity will occur at the end of the century.
4. Some scientists imagine a peaceful future where humans enjoy more leisure time.

B

1. mathematician	**2.** upgrade
3. evolved	**4.** exist

Do you want to live forever?

Useful Expressions p. 24

B

1. in 2. out 3. across
4. over 5. by

Listening p. 25

Script

A: I'm so frustrated. My parents refuse to learn how to use a computer, so I have to call them long distance all the time.

B: Come on, Marie. It can't be that bad. How much is your phone bill?

A: Three hundred and three dollars!

B: Whoa, that's really high! You could buy a computer for that amount of money.

A: I know, but they're scared of computers. My dad's afraid he will delete an important file or something. And my mom doesn't even want to learn how to turn it on!

B: How did they go this long without using a computer?

A: Well, my father worked in construction for most of his life. It wasn't necessary for him to use a computer. My mom took care of the house and the kids while my dad was at work.

B: Have you or your siblings tried to teach them?

A: Of course. Three years ago my brother, my sister, and I pitched in and bought them a really nice laptop for Christmas. My brother set it up for them, including an internet connection and video chat software.

B: What happened?

A: They used it once, and then they never turned it on again. It just sat on a desk for years collecting dust.

B: What are you going to do?

A: I'm going to buy some stamps at the post office.

A

1. over 2. construction 3. three
4. laptop 5. write

B

1. True 2. True 3. False
4. False

Have you seen the movie *A.I.*?

Listening p. 27

Script

A: What's your favorite science-fiction movie that is also a novel, Caleb?

B: Oh, that's easy. I love the movie *Minority Report*. It came out in theaters in 2002. Tom Cruise stars as John Anderton, a police officer in the future. He works for the pre-crime unit in the police department. The pre-crime unit uses humans with special powers to see the future. These special people are called pre-cogs, and they can see the crimes people are going to commit before they actually commit the crimes. John Anderton leads a police force that arrests the people who have committed the crimes in the pre-cogs' visions. Everything is going smoothly until one day when the pre-cogs see a vision of him committing a murder. He knows he isn't capable of committing murder and goes on the run to prove his innocence. The movie is visually exciting, and the story moves at a fast pace. It's directed by Steven Spielberg. I also read the book *The Minority Report* by Philip K. Dick. It was published in 1956 at the height of the Cold War. I was surprised by how different the stories were. In the book, Tom Cruise's character, John Anderton, is married with no children, but in the film, he becomes dedicated to the pre-crime unit six months after the kidnapping and murder of his young son. He believes that the pre-crime unit could have prevented the kidnapping of his son.

A

1. c 2. c 3. b
4. c 5. b

B

The movie title I watched is *Minority Report*. It was released in 2002. The movie is based on the book *The Minority Report*, which was published in 1956.

A Movie Review

Reading p. 28

Comprehension Check

1. Jupiter is a great distance away.
2. HAL controls the ship's operations.
3. HAL wants to complete the secret mission.
4. He cuts its circuits.
5. HAL lacked morality and emotion.

Wrap-up p. 30

A

1. in 2. across 3. by
4. over 5. out 6. on

Unit 3 Different Perspectives

It's cold in here.

Listening p. 33

Script

1. A: I'm so angry at James. I could just scream.

B: What's wrong, Cynthia?

A: James said he would sit down with me on Wednesday to go over our guest lists for the wedding this August. We're only inviting 50 guests in total, so we have to narrow our lists down to 25 each.

B: He doesn't think 25 guests is enough?

A: I have no idea what he thinks because he just blew me off and watched soccer instead.

B: Did you say anything at the time?

A: Of course. I asked him to sit with me at the kitchen table, but he said he wanted to see the end of the soccer match. Barcelona was playing Real Madrid, so he had to watch it.

B: Did you guys discuss the guest lists after the game?

A: After the game, his friend called him to talk about the soccer match. By the time they were finished talking, it was ten o'clock.

B: That's really selfish. Then what did you do?

A: Nothing. I'm not going to nag him about it.

2. A: Cynthia's mad at me.

B: Really? Why?

A: I honestly have no idea.

B: What do you think it might be?

A: Last night, I was watching the soccer game. Did you see it?

B: Of course. Real Madrid won 3–2. It was amazing.

A: She knows I love soccer, and she's never had a problem with me watching a game before. When the game finished, she was really cold.

B: Did anything specific happen after the game?

A: Frank from the office called me at 9:30 p.m. We always chat after big games.

B: Anything else? How about wedding planning? That always involves a lot of details.

A: Oh, right! She wanted to go over the guest lists last night, but I forgot.

B: There you go. She thinks you don't care about the wedding.

A: You're right. What should I do?

B: You'd better get some flowers after work today. And forget about watching soccer for a while.

A

1. a	**2.** b	**3.** c
4. c	**5.** a	

B

1. False	**2.** True	**3.** True
4. True	**5.** False	

My boss is crazy!

Useful Expressions p. 34

B

1. up with	**2.** on	**3.** back/away
4. off		

Listening p. 35

Script

Congratulations on being promoted to management positions. Now that you are managers, I'd like you to consider how your relationships with your former coworkers might change. I've created a five-point plan that each of you should follow.

1. Be humble. Don't flaunt your new position or talk about it with the people in your office. And never discuss your salary with your workers!
2. Be prepared to feel lonely. You are no longer just a team member, but you're now a leader. In baseball, the coach doesn't go out for drinks with the players after a game. The best coaches keep their distance, and they do it for good reason.
3. Get organized. Because there might be some bitterness in the office, some of the workers might secretly like to see you fail as a manager. This is not a personal attack on you. Win them over by running a well-organized office.
4. Be assertive. Just because you used to be friendly with your workers doesn't mean they have the right to walk all over you. Be strict but fair with your workforce.
5. Set a good example. Be on time, stay focused, and keep the lines of communication open with your staff. The best way to win over your workers is by showing them you're a competent leader.

A

1. b	**2.** c	**3.** a
4. a	**5.** b	

B

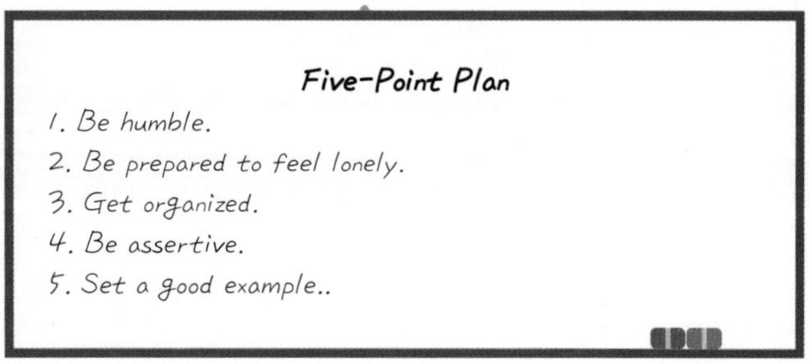

This room is too dirty.

Vocabulary p. 36

1. d	**2.** a	**3.** c
4. e	**5.** f	**6.** b

Listening p. 37

Script

A: Room service is taking way too long. I ordered our hamburgers at 5:00 p.m.!

B: It's only 5:10. How fast do you expect them to be?

A: This room is $200 a night. I expect them to be really fast.

B: I don't think you're being fair.

A: And they only gave us two towels. That's ridiculous.

B: There are extra towels in the wooden pantry. It also has extra toilet paper, shampoo, and toothpaste.

A: Well, the view isn't very nice. It's too dark outside.

B: It's cloudy. You can't blame the hotel for the weather, can you?

A: I guess not.

B: Tomorrow, the view of Miami Beach will be beautiful. I checked the weather app on my phone. It'll be hot and sunny, and there will be a high of 30 degrees. You'd better wear some sunscreen.

A: Oh, great. I forgot my sunscreen!

B: Check the pantry. I saw a small tube in there.

A: I guess this hotel is okay.

B: And there's our food. Only 15 minutes. That's pretty fast if you ask me.

A: Great. I'm starving. I haven't eaten since noon.

A

1. False	2. True	3. True
4. False	5. True	

B

3

The 5 Love Languages

Reading p. 38

Comprehension Check

1. She writes weekly articles.
2. It came out 25 years ago.
3. gift giving, physical touching, words of affirmation, acts of service, and quality time
4. Her love language is gift giving. His love language is acts of service.

Wrap-up p. 40

A

1. up with	2. away	3. down
4. off	5. back	6. on

Unit 4 Mysteries

He believes in Bigfoot.

Vocabulary p. 42

1. Bigfoot	2. Loch Ness Monster
3. poltergeist	4. fortunetelling
5. reincarnation	6. Martian

Listening p. 43

Script

A: Have you ever seen the television show *Ghost Hunters*? It's on Friday evenings at eleven o'clock.

B: No, I haven't. My boyfriend and I always go out then.

A: My wife and I love horror movies and reality TV, so this show is perfect for us.

B: What's it about?

A: It's a documentary series that follows a group of experts in the paranormal as they travel to haunted locations around the United States and try to capture images or record the voices of ghosts by using very sensitive equipment.

B: What do you mean by paranormal?

A: Paranormal means strange or unexplainable. Last week's episode was really intense. They went to the Myrtles Plantation in Louisiana. People say it's one of the most haunted locations in the world. They believe there are more than ten ghosts there.

B: I've got goosebumps. So what happened? Did they record any ghost sounds?

A: Their equipment recorded some unusual sounds, but they didn't see any actual ghosts.

B: You must really believe in this stuff, huh?

A: I really do.

A

1. b	2. c	3. a
4. b		

B

1. The woman and her boyfriend always go out on Friday nights.
2. The man and his wife enjoy horror movies and reality TV.
3. The ghost hunters recorded sounds of a ghost.
4. The Myrtles Plantation is one of the most haunted locations in the world.

Have you ever seen a UFO?

Useful Expressions p. 44

B

1. saw	2. touched	3. felt
4. looked	5. smelled	

Listening p. 45

Script

A: Jiyoung, would you please share your fascinating UFO story with us today?

B: Sure, I'd be happy to. About three years ago, my friend and I were hanging out on the patio in her backyard. We were drinking margaritas and talking about our love lives. We were complaining about our boyfriends. Ha-ha! Then, the strangest thing happened. While I was mixing drinks in the kitchen,

I heard my friend shriek. I was so surprised by her scream that I spilled a drink on the floor of the kitchen. I ran outside to see what the problem was, and there they were, three UFOs about thirty meters above the ground in her backyard. We were frozen by the sight of these spaceships. They were unlike anything we'd ever seen in our lives. I've told this story to countless friends, and they always say it was probably an airplane, a helicopter, or a drone. No! It was none of those things. They were flying saucers! They were just floating there with these beautiful lights emanating from them. They floated there for about thirty seconds, and then they just zoomed away. I took out my phone and tried to snap a picture, but I was too late. All you can see in the picture is a faint stream of light. My friend and I know they were UFOs, but the picture doesn't prove it. I just wish I'd taken a picture a second earlier.

A

1. Jiyoung spilled a drink on the kitchen floor.
2. Jiyoung witnessed three UFOs in the sky.
3. Jiyoung and her friend were talking on the patio of her house.
4. Jiyoung and her friend watched the UFOs for 30 seconds.

B

1. three UFOs
2. in friend's backyard
3. drinking a margarita, talking
4. amazed

Is there life on other planets?

Group Work p. 46

1.

The Bermuda Triangle	
What happened?	Ships and airplanes went missing in this particular region of the ocean.
When did it happen?	People began noticing strange disappearances in the region approximately one-hundred years ago.
Where did it happen?	The disappearances occured in the western region of the North Atlantic Ocean.

2.

Atlantis	
What happened?	An entire island was thought to have sunk in the ocean.
When did it happen?	It happened about 9,000 years before Plato wrote about it.
Where did it happen?	The island was thought to have been in the middle of the Atlantic Ocean.

3.

Area 51	
What happened?	An alien crash-landed on Earth.
When did it happen?	It occurred in 1947.
Where did it happen?	The crash occurred in Roswell, New Mexico. But conspiracy theorists believe the alien's body and spacecraft were transported to a U.S. air force base in the Nevada desert.

Listening p. 47

Script

1. There is an island off the coast of Chile in the Pacific Ocean named Easter Island, and it is home to some of the world's most fascinating stone figures. The stone figures reach heights of four meters and weigh up to fourteen tons. There are more than 900 figures on the island, and experts believe that they were put there more than 1,000 years ago. How would the inhabitants of this region be able to move large statues such great distances without the assistance of modern tools or machines? One explanation suggests that they did so with the help of advanced alien technology. Alien theorists hypothesize that the aliens shared secret technology with the inhabitants that allowed them to move the giant stone objects. The statues, they believe, are a tribute to the aliens for their technological gifts.
2. I want to discuss a very interesting location called Stonehenge. Stonehenge is located in the English countryside of Salisbury and consists of large stacked pillars arranged in a circle, with some of the stones weighing up to fifty tons each. Those who believe in the alien explanation for the structure believe that the stone monuments were built by aliens and served as a landing pad or launching pad for alien spacecraft. When we think about the physical attributes of a UFO—circular and able to hover above the ground—the appeal of the landing pad or launching pad theory becomes more attractive. Of course, this is all fun speculation. Some researchers have suggested that Stonehenge was built by the Druids more than a thousand years ago; however, most archaeologists believe the structure is much older than the Druids. Carbon dating estimates the structure to be 5,000 years old.

A

1. a 2. c 3. c
4. a

B

1. Easter Island, more than 1,000 years ago
2. Stonehenge, 5,000 years ago

The Pyramids and Orion's Belt

Reading p. 48

Comprehension Check

1. It allowed the person safe passage into the afterlife.
2. They look in the ground and try to unearth ancient artifacts that have been slowly buried over thousands of years.
3. They lined up with Orion's belt.
4. Osiris was the god of the underworld and could allow safe passage into the afterlife.

Wrap-up p. 50

A

1. Loch Ness Monster
2. Martians
3. poltergeist
4. Bigfoot
5. reincarnation
6. Fortunetelling

B

1. watched	2. felt	3. looked
4. touched	5. smelled	6. heard

Unit 5 Priorities

She thinks I work too much.

Listening p. 53

Script

A: I don't know what to do. My husband just called to tell me that his boss and his boss's wife want to take us out to dinner tonight, but I want to see the movie *Heartbeats* with my sister.

B: That's a tough situation. When did you make plans with your sister?

A: I called her on Wednesday to see if she wanted to go. She said yes, so we already bought the tickets online.

B: When does the movie start?

A: It starts at nine o'clock, but she wants to meet in front of the theater at eight thirty. And the dinner's at eight o'clock.

B: You have to cancel with your sister.

A: Do you really think so?

B: Your husband's job is more important than a movie with your sister.

A: What do you mean?

B: He can't go to the restaurant by himself. It would be uncomfortable for the three of them.

A: I guess you're right. What about my sister and the movie tickets?

B: Your sister is single, isn't she?

A: So?

B: I'm single.

A: You want to go out with my sister?

B: You brought her as your plus-one to our company's Christmas party last year. I thought she was really cute.

A: All right. I've got to talk to her first to see if she's interested.

A

1. b	2. a	3. c
4. c		

B

1. Her husband's boss invited her and her husband to dinner.
2. The woman and her sister bought tickets online.
3. The man is interested in dating the woman's sister.
4. The woman brought her sister to the Christmas party last year.

Here's what you should do.

Useful Expressions p. 54

B

1. a hotel, a flight
2. tasks, time
3. travel expenses, an application
4. a note, a newsletter

C

process, book, prioritize, write

Listening p. 55

Script

Monday, March 17th, to-do list: breakfast meeting at Park Avenue Grill at 8:00 a.m. You are meeting with Simon and Natasha to discuss the 12th Avenue hotel development project. Email the cost projections to them tonight, but also print out hard copies for them. Set aside ten minutes to discuss the office building project in SoHo. Next, ask your assistant to set up a lunch meeting for next week with Mr. Williams and the CEO to discuss the 12th Avenue hotel development project. Things to discuss include the addition of a rooftop swimming pool and relevant zoning regulations associated with that. You should also discuss the construction of an additional level of underground parking. Current designs include three levels of basement parking, but new zoning laws allow for four levels of underground parking. Cost projections for one additional level of parking come out to 1.2 million dollars. After lunch, you have a 3:30 meeting with the legal department to discuss safety regulations regarding the construction of the office building in SoHo. Ask the legal department about the current safety regulations for a construction project near a subway station entrance. At seven o'clock, you are meeting Janine at Splendor for cocktails. Be home by nine o'clock in order to finish the report for the SoHo project. Be asleep by midnight! No TV!

A

1. c 2. b 3. c
4. c

B

8:00 a.m.	breakfast with Simon and Natasha
Lunchtime	meeting with Mr. Williams and CEO
3:30 p.m.	meeting with legal department
7:00 p.m.	drinks with Janine
9:00 p.m.	finishing SoHo report

I need a little more "me" time.

Listening p. 57

Script

Last Friday, I took a day off from work in order to do all of the things that I like to do. My morning started with my favorite drink at my favorite coffee shop. I ordered a chai tea latte with sugar and a banana nut muffin. I read a magazine while I drank my tea and ate my muffin. I was in heaven. After that, I went to the spa. I had scheduled a massage for ten o'clock but I arrived at the spa at nine. I decided to spend half an hour in the sauna before my massage. At ten o'clock, I got my massage from Sven, my favorite masseuse. He is so talented. When the massage was finished, I spent some time in the hot tub. I left the spa at eleven thirty because I had a lunch date with my best friend Susan. We met at Picante, my favorite Mexican restaurant, at twelve o'clock. I ordered the quesadillas and the vegetarian tacos. Susan ordered the Mexican salad and chicken tacos. This restaurant gives you free chips and salsa sauce, so I was already full when my food arrived. Susan and I brought our leftovers home with us from the restaurant. After lunch, we saw a movie at the local movie theater. We saw the latest Brad Pitt movie. Susan and I think he is so handsome! After the movie, Susan and I drank cocktails at this cute little bar by the beach. We talked for hours and had such a nice time. At about eight o'clock, I said goodbye to Susan and went home. My husband and children were eating pizza and watching a movie in the living room when I got home. I went to the bedroom and finished my leftovers from Picante while I watched my favorite drama on television. I must say it was a perfect day!

A

1. c 2. c 3. b
4. a

B

Morning: went to a coffee shop, got a massage
Afternoon: ate lunch, saw a movie
Evening: drank cocktails, watched her favorite drama

It's as Simple as ABC!

Reading p. 58

Comprehension Check

1. He learned it from his freshman year college counselor.
2. He has used it since he learned about it in college.
3. They are urgent tasks that must be done immediately.
4. Focus on the B list, tackle the A list as soon as one comes up, and pay little to no attention to the C list.

Wrap-up p. 60

A

Dear Mr. Seung,

I am writing this email because I ~~wanna~~ want to confirm our meeting for next week. I also hope your trip to China went well. ~~Didja~~ Did you have a chance to meet with the factory manager? Do you think they will be able to manufacture our semiconductors for the amount we discussed? In our meeting next week, we ~~hafta~~ have to discuss the budget for our next project. I'm ~~gonna~~ going to bring my notes from my meeting with our U.S. client when we meet next week. I've ~~gotta~~ got to talk to Mr. Simmons in the U.S. office about some minor details regarding the new project before we meet. I'll let you know when I've spoken to Mr. Simmons.

Sincerely,

John Rand
Project Manager of SB Corp.

B

1. prioritize 2. book 3. process
4. book 5. write 6. prioritize

Unit 6 Genetics

Warm-up p. 61

1. wholphin 2. Savannah
3. grolar bear 4. cama
5. liger 6. zebroid
7. mule 8. beefalo
9. zebroid 10. mule
11. liger

Am I losing my hair?

Words Search Puzzle p. 62

s	s	l	x	q	w	s	d	g	i
o	p	a	o	r	g	a	n	s	n
f	o	b	g	u	y	j	o	c	h
f	e	o	a	g	i	n	g	f	e
s	m	r	w	d	c	l	q	s	r
p	b	a	y	a	j	i	n	a	i
r	r	t	k	c	l	o	n	e	t
i	y	o	k	l	r	q	s	a	e
n	o	r	s	c	d	n	a	c	d
g	a	y	f	f	s	c	y	x	a

1. clone
2. aging
3. inherited
4. offspring
5. embryo
6. laboratory

Listening p. 63

Script

A: Is that a picture of your family, Pablo?

B: Yes, it is.

A: You look like your mother.

B: Do you think so?

A: You have the same brown eyes as her.

B: I think you're right. But I have my father's curly hair.

A: Yes, that's true. And you're tall like him.

B: Who do you look like, Amber, your mother or your father?

A: Well, I'm kind of a combination of both although I probably look more like my mom than my dad. I've got my dad's blue eyes, but I have my mom's red hair.

B: One of your sisters has red hair, too, right?

A: Marlene has long, straight red hair. It looks exactly like our mother's. She also has green eyes like our mother. But my hair is wavy like my dad's.

B: And your eyes are blue, not green.

A: Right. I'm a mix of both of them, I guess.

B: What about your other sister, Tiffany?

A: She's the real beauty in the family. She's got our father's blue eyes and blonde hair. My father has gray hair now, but it was blond when he was younger.

B: I'll bet she's quite popular on campus.

A: She is. She's got a handsome boyfriend. They've been dating for three years. I wouldn't be surprised if they got married after graduation.

A

1. The woman thinks Pablo looks similar to his mother.
2. Pablo is tall and has curly hair.
3. Amber looks more like her mom than her dad.
4. Amber thinks Tiffany is the most beautiful of her sisters.
5. Tiffany and her boyfriend have been dating for three years.

B

1. Tiffany
2. Amber
3. Marlene

Designer Babies

Useful Expressions p. 64

B

1. What do you mean by
2. Excuse me.
3. Why do you say that?, Pardon me?

Listening p. 65

Script

A: I am Christina Kim, a staff writer for *Science Monthly magazine*, and I'm speaking to Dr. Jennifer Copeland from the American Institute of the Sciences. Dr. Copeland, what can you tell us about the term designer babies?

B: Designer babies is a term that refers to genetically changing a human embryo in order to give it the most desirable genetic traits.

A: Is it easy to modify genes?

B: No, not at all. People's understanding of the hard science surrounding gene manipulation has been blurred by television and movies. People think it's a simple process and that we're far more advanced than we actually are. But it's true that we are moving toward a future where genetic modification will become a normal occurrence.

A: Why is it so difficult to modify genes?

B: There are just so many genes responsible for determining who we are. Trying to isolate one to change it is very difficult. However, lots of research is being done in the field right now. Scientists have made huge advances by using a technology called CRSPR. It's entirely possible that we will one day be able to modify embryos by giving them amazing genetic traits. But it will be something that happens in the distant future.

A: What are scientists able to do now? What is the hard science?

B: What we can do now is test embryos for certain desirable traits and then implant the best embryo into the mother's womb. That's hard science because it has been replicated many times in our laboratories by using animals and even humans.

1. b
2. c
3. c
4. b

Stem Cell Therapy

Vocabulary p. 66

1. a genetic disease that results in memory loss and the loss of other cognitive functions
2. a disorder that affects the brain and results in a number of symptoms, such as tremors, balance issues, and slowness of movement
3. a disease that results in blood sugar levels being too high
4. a disease that affects the joints and causes joint pain
5. a central nervous system disease that causes the disruption of signals from the brain to the body
6. a chronic autoimmune disease that causes the body's immune system to attack healthy cells
7. the deterioration of the kidneys
8. the deterioration of the liver
9. the lack of oxygenated blood flowing from the lungs to the brain due to arterial blockage
10. the body's inability to pump oxygenated blood to the body and brain

Listening p. 67

Script

There are more than 30,000 organ transplants performed each year in the United States, and this number is rising. A host of challenges exist for doctors and patients in regards to organ transplantation. For example, there are long waiting lists for patients needing organ transplants, so for older recipients low on the list, this situation can be very stressful and oftentimes deadly. Organ rejection is another common problem associated with organ transplantation. But what if scientists were able to grow an organ in a lab using DNA from a person's body? Well, that's exactly how transplants will most likely occur in the not too distant future. For example, a patient needing a liver transplant will donate a small sample of tissue, and from this tissue, a new liver will be grown in a laboratory. Because the organ grown in the lab contains the exact same DNA as the patient, medications that stop the person's body from rejecting the organ will not be necessary. Growing an organ in a laboratory is also cheaper and more efficient than harvesting an organ from an organ donor. By growing organs in a laboratory, countless numbers of patients will be saved. For aging populations all over the world struggling with organ failure, this news is very exciting.

A

1. a 2. b 3. a
4. b

Are You a Super-Sleeper?

Reading p. 68

Comprehension Check

1. A short sleeper requires about six hours of sleep per night.
2. They possess the DEC2 gene.
3. High blood pressure, strokes, and heart attacks are associated with a chronic lack of sleep.
4. It gives short-sleepers access to a deeper state of REM sleep.
5. Scientists will find a way to give everyone the DEC2 mutation.

Report p. 69

The Cloning Debate

This article discusses cloning. The writer describes two versions of cloning. The first is called reproductive cloning. It involves copying one organism's DNA to make another organism that is exactly the same. The second type of cloning is therapeutic cloning. It involves using a sick person's DNA to create a new organ which can be transplanted into the body of the sick person. A benefit of therapeutic cloning is that the lab-grown organ will be a perfect match for the recipient. Therapeutic cloning may become the most important medical breakthrough in decades.

Wrap-up p. 70

A

1. clone 2. offspring
3. embryo 4. DNA
5. aging 6. inherited gene

B

1. Excuse me., Pardon me?
2. Why do you say that?
3. What do you mean by

Unit 7 Personal Finance

What is the asking price?

Vocabulary p. 72

A

1. mortgage
2. fixed rate mortgage
3. adjustable rate mortgage
4. asking price
5. government subsidy
6. crunch numbers

Listening p. 73

Script

A: Welcome to 1st National Bank. I'm Erika Winters, the loan officer at this branch. How may I help you?

B: Hello. My name is John Jacobs, and I'd like to apply for a loan.

A: Oh, okay. So what kind of loan are you seeking?

B: I want to buy another truck for my business.

A: Okay, so is this a small business loan then?

B: Yes, that's right. The truck costs $30,000. So are you going to give me cash or write me a check?

A: First, I need to ask you some questions regarding your financial situation before we can approve you for a loan.

B: Oh, okay, I see. What do you need to know?

A: I'd like to know what amount of personal debt you have in the forms of mortgages, car loans, or any other loans that you're currently paying back. I'd also like to know if you have any credit card debt.

B: Well, let me see. My wife and I owe $250,000 on our house and an additional $100,000 on our cabin. I took out a personal loan last year for a motorcycle. That was $30,000. We have about $45,000 in credit card debt.

A: I see. And have you defaulted on any of these loans?

B: I've missed a few credit card payments in the past year. My business isn't doing so well, you see. That's why I need a second truck.

A: I'm really sorry, but I'm afraid we have to deny you this loan. You have $425,000 of debt and substandard credit.

A

1. The man is interested in buying a new truck.
2. The man is applying for a small business loan.
3. The man and his wife own a house and a cabin.
4. The loan officer won't approve the man's loan.

B

Personal Debt: $425,000
Requested Loan Amount: $30,000
Credit Rating: ☐ excellent ☐ good ☐ fair ☑ poor ☐ other
Loan Officer's Decision: ☐ approved ☑ denied

Credit Card Debt

Vocabulary p. 74

1. magnetic strip
2. interest rate
3. credit card number
4. credit card company
5. credit card reader
6. credit card statement

Listening p. 75

Script

A: I'm really in a financial mess, sis. I've got $30,000 in credit card debt.

B: How did that happen?

A: I don't know. It started with one credit card and spiraled out of control.

B: How many cards do you have?

A: I've got five cards now, so 30% of my salary goes toward the minimum payments. It's about $600 per month.

B: Daniel Steven Fullerton! How could you? You have to do something about this problem.

A: Do you think it's a good idea for me to pay off all of my credit card debt by using one new card with a 7% annual interest rate.

B: What are the interest rates on your other cards?

A: The lowest one is 6.5%, and the highest one is 8%.

B: I don't think it's a good idea. Your problem is not the multiple cards. Your problem is your spending habits. You need to make a monthly budget, and you need to stick to it.

A: What do you mean?

B: You need to stop going out on the weekends. Every time we meet at a bar, you start buying people rounds of drinks.

A: I guess you're right. I do have a tendency to get out of control with my spending.

A

1. a 2. c 3. b

B

Cardholder's Name: Mr. Daniel S. Fullerton
Number of Credit Cards: 5
Amount of Debt: $30,000
Minimum Monthly Payments Due: $600 per month

Should I cosign the loan?

Grammar p. 76

B

1. hope 2. wish 3. wishes
4. hopes 5. wishes

Listening p. 77

Script

A: Welcome back to *Truth Talk*. I'm your host, Mira Swanson. With more than 30 years of experience in the finance industry, I am prepared to provide you with sound financial advice. Tonight, we have a caller on the show, Mr. Donald Lee, from Tampa, Florida. Thank you for joining us tonight, Donald.

B: Thank you, Mira.

A: So tell us a bit about your financial situation.

B: My wife and I have about $20,000 in credit card debt and another $10,000 in car debt. We bought our house for $200,000 fifteen years ago, but now it's worth approximately $250,000; however, we still owe almost $150,000 on it. In total, we have about $180,000 of debt.

A: Now, let's talk about your salaries. How much money do you and your wife earn?

B: We take home about $8,500 per month.

A: In the past fifteen years, you've only paid off $50,000 of your mortgage. What that tells me is that your spending habits are not healthy. You definitely shouldn't have any credit card debt or car debt. If you're going to buy a car, you need to pay for it in cash. So what I want you to do is to set aside $2,000 per month for your credit card debt. Pay that off first. In about ten months, it will be gone. I also want you to set aside $1,000 per month for your car debt. That will also be paid off in ten months. You and your wife will have to pay the rest of your monthly bills by using the leftover $5,500. When ten months have passed and your credit card debt and car payments are completed, I want you to put that $3,000 per month toward your mortgage. In fewer than five years, you and your wife will be completely debt free. Do you think you and your wife can follow that plan, Donald?

B: Yes, I do. Thank you, Mira!

A

1. c	2. b	3. b
4. a	5. a	

B

Current Mortgage Balance: $150,000
Credit Cards: $20,000
Car Debt: $10,000
Total Debt: $180,000

Dear Mom and Dad

Reading p. 78

Comprehension Check

1. She has no money to pay for her car or her rent, and she lost her job.
2. The car was making a loud noise.
3. Her name wasn't on the lease.
4. She gets paid less.
5. She will feel very relieved.

Wrap-up p. 80

A

1. mortgage
2. interest rate
3. credit card number
4. credit card statement
5. crunch
6. credit card reader

B

1. wishes	2. hopes	3. hopes
4. wish	5. wishes	

Unit 8 Emergencies

I smell smoke.

Vocabulary p. 82

1. h	2. e	3. g
4. d	5. i	6. f
7. c	8. a	9. b

Listening p. 83

Script

A: Is that the new PR6 phone?

B: Yeah, I just bought it.

A: Haven't you seen the news reports?

B: What news reports?

A: The PR6 has a problem with its battery.

B: Is the battery life really short with this model?

A: No, that's not the problem.

B: What is it then?

A: The batteries have been catching on fire.

B: Are you serious? I had a PR5 for a year and a half, and I didn't have any problems with the battery.

A: The problem is only with the newest PR6 models. Apparently, the batteries can overheat and catch on fire. It can be really dangerous if the phone is in a person's pocket.

B: What am I going to do? This cost me $700. I can't afford to throw it away.

A: You don't have to. The company is doing a full recall. Just go to the shop where you bought it, and you can exchange it for a different model or get a refund.

B: Really? I'm so relieved. Thank you for telling me.

A: No problem. I just want you to be safe.

A

1. b	2. a	3. b
4. a		

B

1. True	2. False	3. False
4. True		

Somebody call 911!

Listening p. 85

Script

A: Thank you for attending our annual meeting of emergency medical technicians, EMTs. Today, we're going to listen to a personal story from heart attack survivor Walter Peterson. Please give a nice round of applause to Walter, everyone.

B: Thank you, Melinda. Three years ago, I had a heart attack. The day of my heart attack started like any other day of the week. It was about ten in the morning, and my wife and I were working in the garden. We are both retired, so we spend a lot of time in our garden. On this particular day, I was having some shoulder pain. I thought nothing of it because I had been pulling weeds for a couple of hours by then. I decided to take some pain medicine, but the pain became worse, and I started experiencing shooting pain down the left side of my arm. My wife became very worried. Before she could even ask me if I wanted to go to the hospital, I was unconscious. I was having a massive heart attack. All four arteries to my heart were blocked, and I was only 65 years old. My wife called 911, and within two minutes, EMTs Julia and Kim were working on me. They knew exactly what to do. Kim began chest compressions, and Julia delivered oxygen to my lungs through a mask. They continued this process the entire length of the journey to the hospital. Julia and Kim kept me alive long enough for the ER doctors to take over. A few minutes after arriving at the hospital, the doctors restarted my heart. The only reason they were able to save me is the incredibly fast response and skilled care of EMTs Julia and Kim. It took three months for me to recover from my heart surgery. Now I take care of my body and eat a healthy diet. But none of that would have been possible without my EMTs. I owe my life to them. So please believe me when I say your work is the most important work, and although patients may not always be good at expressing their gratitude, we are so very thankful for the work you do.

A

1. c 2. b 3. b
4. c 5. a

B

Medical Condition: heart attack
EMT Response Time: 2 minutes
Who did what: Julia or Kim?
Did Chest Compressions: Kim
Gave Oxygen: Julia
Walter's Recovery Time: 3 months

This is a fire drill!

Grammar p. 86

B

1. He finally persuaded the teacher to give him an extra week to hand in the assignment.
2. My trainer encourages me to work harder during our training sessions.
3. Minsoo would like you to meet him at the airport.
4. The snow caused traffic to slow down immensely.
5. We need everyone to remain calm!

Listening p. 87

Script

Good morning, everyone! I've been asked to discuss with you the appropriate actions to take in case of an emergency. If there is a fire, we all need to move toward the east exit and use the eastern stairwell. The western stairwell is reserved for workers working on the 21st to 40th floors. But those working on the 1st to 20th floors must use the east exit. If everyone in the building were to use the same staircase, it could cause major delays in getting people out of the building and perhaps result in injury or even death. And I'm also supposed to tell you that in case of an emergency, no one is to use the elevators. Using the elevators during an emergency could result in an even bigger tragedy because the elevators are programmed to shut down during a fire or severe weather warning. If someone were to become trapped in the elevator, it could be very dangerous, especially if there's a fire. In case there is severe weather such as a tornado, employees are to exit any rooms with large windows and should take cover under desks or large tables. The desks or tables will protect your head from injury in the event that debris is thrown across the room. This Thursday, we are going to have a fire drill at eleven o'clock in the morning. Then, on Friday, there will be a severe weather drill at 2:00 p.m. Dan is going to be in charge of our floor during the drills because I'll be out of town on business. On those days, he will be assisting you with directions, so listen to what he says, and everything will go smoothly. Thank you for your time today.

A

1. b 2. a 3. c
4. c

B

1. False 2. True 3. True
4. True

Survivor's Guilt

Reading p. 88

Comprehension Check

1. Feeling guilty because you were not injured or killed in an accident where other people were
2. They were going to their high school senior prom.
3. Chris and Jenna were in the front seats. Kelly and Max were in the backseats.
4. Chris and Jenna got lots of cuts.

Wrap-up p. 90

A

1. concussion 2. Shallow breathing
3. electrocuted 4. emergency room
5. choking 6. stroke

B

1. We need you to donate food and clothes to the shelter.
2. My father encouraged me to study hard at my university, so I could get a good job.
3. My sister will never persuade me to go skydiving.
4. Do you want me to help you look for a job?
5. I can't believe you got Andy to fly in for Dad's birthday.

Unit 9 Extinction and Endangered Animals

Warm-up p. 91

1. dodo: extinct
2. orangutan: endangered
3. rhinoceros: endangered
4. sea turtle: endangered
5. mammoth: extinct
6. Narwhal: not endangered, but near threatened
7. grand Cayman blue iguana: endangered
8. Tasmanian tiger: extinct

The Tasmanian Tiger

Vocabulary p. 92

1. f	2. e	3. b
4. a	5. c	6. d

Listening p. 93

Script

A: Do you want to hear something really interesting?

B: Sure.

A: Scientists think they can create a mammoth embryo by using DNA from the carcass of a frozen mammoth found in Siberia. They will extract DNA from the frozen mammoth and then use that to create a baby mammoth.

B: Where will the mammoth embryo grow without a mother?

A: They're going to implant the mammoth embryo into a female Asian elephant.

B: That's incredible. But why are they bringing mammoths back? Why not the dodo or the passenger pigeon?

A: That's the most interesting part. This scientist who is doing research in Siberia about the melting polar ice caps believes we can slow the melting by letting mammoths roam the countryside of Siberia.

B: That sounds crazy.

A: I know, but hear me out. One of the reasons it's getting warmer in the Arctic region is that dead trees and plants are creating a protective layer on the ground like a blanket. It's causing the ice deep in the ground to melt and release harmful gases like methane into our atmosphere.

B: But how would bringing mammoths back from extinction help?

A: When mammoths roamed Siberia thousands of years ago, they used to dig under the snow with their tusks and eat the plants. Without a layer of plants and trees on the ground, more of the earth was exposed to the cold Arctic temperatures.

B: And because more of the ground was frozen, harmful gases like methane remained trapped in the dirt and ice far below the surface of the earth.

A

1. b	2. c	3. a

B

1. True	2. False	3. False
4. True		

Why don't we make a donation?

Pair Work p. 94

1. The Pinta Island tortoise lived in the Island of Pinta in the Galapagos Islands. It became endangered by the middle of the 19th century because of hunting. Conservationists attempted to mate the last one with a compatible female, but the female produced no viable eggs. It was classified as extinct in June 24th, 2012.
2. The West African black rhinoceros lived in the southeastern region of Africa. In the early 1900s, it became endangered because of overhunting, poaching, and killing by farmers. Efforts to stop overhunting began in the 1930s. Unfortunately, protection of the animal became too relaxed. The West African black rhinoceros was classified as extinct in the early 2000s.

Listening p. 95

Script

Let's talk about the passenger pigeon for a few minutes. The passenger pigeon, or Ectopistes Migratorius, was the most abundant species of bird in North America when European settlers started arriving during the 1600s. By the late 1890s, however, there were only a few hundred passenger pigeons left. Nearly all of the species had been wiped out. And by 1914, the very last passenger pigeon died in the Cincinnati Zoo. Her name was Martha, and she had been unable to lay one fertile egg in her 29 years of existence. The plight of the passenger pigeon can be attributed to human excess. In the 1600s, the passenger pigeon was perhaps the most successful species of bird to ever live. It traveled in such enormous numbers that when a flock passed over a town, the sky would turn dark. It has been written that the nesting grounds of passenger pigeons were so heavily populated by the birds that tree branches collapsed under the weight of the nests. What made the passenger pigeon so strong in previous generations became its biggest liability as humans moved west across North America. You see, because passenger pigeons traveled in such large flocks, they were very easy to kill. They tasted delicious, too. Hunters would collect barrel upon barrel of passenger pigeons and ship them all over the United States by train. In the span of a few hundred years, the passenger pigeon population went from three billion down to several hundred. And by 1914, they were all gone. But the story of the passenger pigeon may not be over yet. Scientists are considering an attempt to bring the passenger pigeon back by using genetic samples of dead passenger pigeon DNA.

A

1. The passenger pigeon was the most abundant species of bird in North America.
2. Martha lived to be 29 years old and laid zero fertile eggs.
3. Passenger pigeons traveled in large flocks.
4. The passenger pigeon was very easy to hunt.
5. Scientists may attempt to bring the passenger pigeon back by using dead DNA tissue.

B

1. passenger pigeon
2. three billion
3. several hundred
4. 1914

The Human Threat

Listening p. 97

Script

Many of us think of the word extinction as being a negative one. But in the case of infectious diseases, extinction would actually be a blessing to millions of children across the globe. Infectious diseases such as measles and rubella, at one time in history, tormented children in all regions of the world. Today, these diseases have mostly been eradicated from wealthy countries; however, they still linger on in poorer countries, especially those that cannot provide clean drinking water and sanitary conditions to their people. Let's talk about two of these diseases now. First, let's take a look at the measles. The measles has been all but eradicated from the developed world through the use of vaccines. Part of a child's regular vaccination schedule includes a vaccination for the measles. The measles is a disease that can cause blindness, diarrhea, breathing problems, and brain swelling. In some cases, the measles can weaken the immune systems of the children for years, causing a host of medical problems for the child. Now, let's discuss rubella. Rubella is a very contagious virus that in adults can cause a rash to form all over the body as well as cold-like symptoms to occur. In adults, rubella usually clears within a few days; however, in fetuses, the disease is deadly. A fetus that has contracted rubella and survives may experience deafness, blindness, or brain damage, making rubella an extremely dangerous virus. Recently, rubella was declared eradicated from the Americas.

A

1. b 2. b 3. c
4. a

B

1. blindness
2. brain
3. immune systems
4. rash
5. deafness
6. damage

How Did the Dinosaurs Go Extinct?

Reading p. 98

Comprehension Check

1. He presented the asteroid impact and the volcanic eruptions theories.
2. He was interested in which theory the professor thought was more likely true.
3. The iridium dates back 65 million years, the same time as the asteroid impact. And the amount of iridium found in the earth matches the amount in a meteorite.
4. He thinks they were wiped out by volcanic eruptions.
5. He is willing to make the best decision possible with the evidence he has been given.

Wrap-up p. 100

A

1. endangered species
2. conservation
3. polar ice caps
4. extinction, climate change
5. ozone layer

B

1. down the line
2. right now
3. these days
4. lately
5. in the near future

Unit 10 Taking Risks

Warm-up p. 101

A

1. ER / PR
2. PhR
3. PR
4. ER
5. PhR
6. PhR / PR

Facing Your Fears

Listening p. 103

Script

A: This is the Bob Lemke Adventure Podcast, and we have accomplished 17-year-old mountain climber Suyoung Park with us today. So how does it feel to be the youngest female from South Korea to summit Mt. Everest?

B: It feels amazing. And I should mention that not only am I the youngest female from my country to summit Mt. Everest, but I'm also the youngest person from my country to summit Mt. Everest.

A: That's a remarkable feat. Have you climbed any other mountains around the world?

B: Yes, I have. I climbed Denali in Alaska, Kilimanjaro in Africa, and Aconcagua in Chile.

A: When did you first get into climbing?

B: My father's a climber, so he took me to the club when I was young. I used to watch him go up and down the walls.

A: Climbing Mt. Everest is extremely dangerous, so how did you convince your parents to let you go?

B: Summiting Everest was a dream my father and I have shared for a few years. He and I always climb together. He's an excellent mountaineer, too. But my mother hated the idea. She thought it was too dangerous. It took my father almost a year to convince her to let us go.

A: How was he finally able to convince her?

B: Ha-ha-ha! He bribed her. She's hated our kitchen for a long time, so my father renovated the whole thing with a new table and new cupboards. He even bought her a new refrigerator!

A

1. c 2. b 3. a
4. a

B

1. False 2. False 3. True

I finally quit.

Crossword Puzzle p. 104

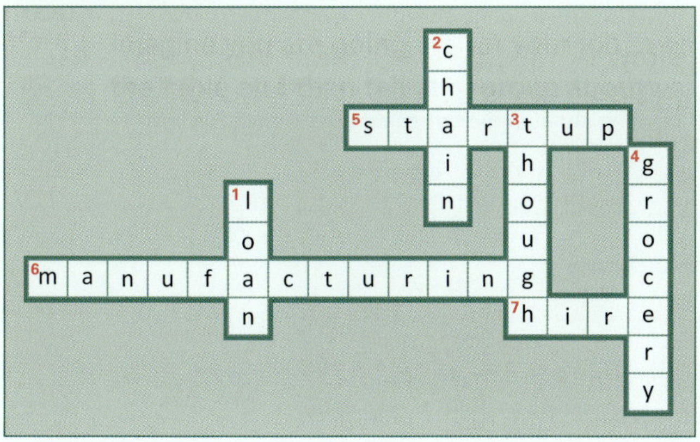

Listening p. 105

Script

Hello. My name is Bernadette Price. I am an entrepreneur and author, and today I want to talk to you about my newest book, *Risking It All: The Right Way to Start a Business.* In *Risking It All*, I've outlined three important pieces of advice that I think all entrepreneurs who are trying to get their startup off the ground should follow. The first one is "Do your homework!" Lots of people have lots of good ideas all the time. But having an idea isn't good enough. Have you made a budget? Is there a market for your product? What is your profit margin? Where are you going to sell your product? Is the market saturated? What makes your product stand out among the others? If you fail to plan, you plan to fail! The second piece of advice is to follow Bernadette's 50/50 principle. If you are not personally invested in at least 50% of your own startup, you're not ready to begin. Oftentimes, those who want to start a business borrow money from family, friends, or the bank. Then, when it doesn't work out, their personal relationships or their credit are left in shambles. You need to have some skin in the game! If you won't invest in yourself, why should anyone else? My last piece of advice is to be sure that you have a good product. Really look at your product, but be objective. Is it useful? Is it cost-effective to produce? Have you done the necessary research and development in order to create the best product possible? If you can say yes to these questions, then perhaps you're ready to sell it.

A

1. b 2. b 3. c
4. c

B

Doing your homework, following Bernadette's 50/50 principle, and having a good product

Is your father feeling better?

Grammar p. 106

B

1. should have come
2. would have joined
3. Wouldn't, have been
4. must have been
5. could have spoken

Listening p. 107

Script

1. Hey, guys! I'm Wendy, and I'm 24 years old. Two years ago, I got a job offer right out of university to teach at a prestigious private high school in upstate New York. I turned it down because my dream has always been to go to graduate school

at NYU. But looking back, I think I made a huge mistake. The private school was going to pay me upward of $50,000 per year and give me a free place to stay on the campus. Instead, I took out a loan for $100,000 and went to graduate school. Graduate school was an awesome experience, but now that I'm done with those two years, I have a master's degree in education, but I also have huge debt and no job! I really wish I could go back in time two years and tell my younger self to take that job in upstate New York.

2. Hey, everyone! I'm Chao, and about three years ago, I dropped out of college to start my own tech company named VRB. VRB stands for Virtual Reality Boardroom. Employees of companies that purchase our software and VR glasses have access to a virtual boardroom where their employees can meet and conduct business from almost anywhere in the world. Unlike a traditional conference call, VRB makes you feel like you're in the room with the person. In the beginning, it was difficult to keep the company afloat, but now I have more than fifty employees, and my company is valued at more than 40 million dollars. Dropping out was a big risk, but it was the best decision I've ever made. I'm a millionaire, and I'm only 22 years old!

1. b 2. b 3. False
4. False 5. b 6. b
7. True 8. False

Michaela's Jujitsu School

Reading p. 108

Comprehension Check

1. She started when she was about twenty years old.
2. She had a small amount of success.
3. It was getting her black belt from Master Cesar De Silva.
4. Her new dream is to open a successful jujitsu academy.
5. She needs students.

Wrap-up p. 110

A

1. startups 2. hire
3. manufacture 4. chains
5. grocery 6. loan

B

1. should have gone
2. would have given
3. couldn't have attended
4. must have opened
5. would, have said

Unit 11 Our Solar System

Warm-up p. 111

A

1. d 2. b 3. a
4. c

There are thousands of other planets.

Build Up Your Knowledge p. 112

1. b 2. a 3. b
4. c 5. a 6. b
7. b 8. a

Listening p. 113

Script

In 2006, the International Astronomical Union, the IAU, released its official definition of a planet. In order for a planet to achieve official status under the IAU, it must meet three requirements. First, a planet must orbit the sun. Second, its mass must be strong enough for it to achieve a round shape. And third, no other objects of comparable size should be in its pathway. If a planet can meet these three criteria, then it can achieve planetary status according to the IAU. And thus began the controversy surrounding Pluto. According to these criteria, Pluto could no longer be considered a planet. Although Pluto meets criteria one and two, it does not meet number three. Pluto's mass is only 0.07 times stronger than some other objects traveling in the same orbit. In comparison, the Earth's mass is many millions of times stronger than that. So, the status of Pluto was officially downgraded to that of a dwarf planet by the IAU. What the IAU wasn't expecting was the emotional attachment that people had formed with the planet Pluto. People were upset that their favorite planet was no longer considered a planet. They received thousands of complaints from outraged people. Those who had lived their entire lives thinking Pluto was a planet felt betrayed. They had learned in elementary school that our solar system contained nine planets, not eight! The state of New Mexico, a southwestern state in the United States, went out of its way to reject the IAU's criteria and declared that Pluto had full planetary status in the state. It's funny how invested people are in this tiny ball of rock and ice floating about in the far reaches of our solar system.

A

1. a 2. b 3. c
4. c

B

1. False 2. False 3. True
4. False

Another NASA Invention

Inventions of NASA p. 114

1, 3, 4, 6, 7, 8

Listening p. 115

Script

A: Do you know who Peggy Whitson is?

B: No, who's that?

A: She's an astronaut. She's third on the list of astronauts with the most spacewalking time.

B: What is spacewalking?

A: Spacewalking is time spent outside the spacecraft.

B: Okay, I see. And how much time did she spend spacewalking?

A: Let's see. Spacepedia.com says that she was out there for 60 hours and 21 minutes in total.

B: Who are number one and number two?

A: Hmm. It says here that Russian cosmonaut Anatoly Solovyev is number one with 82 hours and 22 minutes.

B: That's more than three days!

A: Three and a half, actually. And NASA astronaut Michael Lopez-Alegria spacewalked for 67 hours and 40 minutes.

B: Who's spent the most time in space inside or outside a spacecraft?

A: Oh, some Russian cosmonauts hold the records for the most actual time in space. Valery Polyakov spent 437 days in space. He was part of the Mir Space Station crew. And Sergei Adveyev spent 379 days in space. He was also a part of the Mir Space Station crew. Peggy Whitson has the record for the longest single spaceflight by a woman at 290 days.

B: That's quite impressive. I heard they have a hard time walking when they return to the Earth.

A: Yes. There's no gravity in space, so their muscles become weak. They have to exercise on the space station just to keep their muscles and bones healthy.

A

1. c 2. b 3. b
4. b

B

1. False 2. True 3. False
4. True

A Manned Mission to Mars

Useful Expressions p. 116

B

1. over 2. on 3. out
4. around 5. out 6. up

Listening p. 117

Script

A: We're talking to Dr. Mary-Anne Chang today about the Mars One mission. Could you tell us a bit about this incredible mission to the Red Planet?

B: I'd be happy to. The Mars One mission is a plan to colonize the planet Mars. It is being managed by the Mars One Foundation, a not-for-profit group based in the Netherlands.

A: And how will this plan work?

B: Of course, it's very complicated, but it will essentially begin with a series of unmanned trips to Mars with the supplies necessary to support human life on Mars.

A: How many people does the mission plan to send to Mars?

B: Well, we started with over 200,000 applicants, but it will be narrowed down to just twenty. It will include applicants from all over the world with backgrounds in different fields, such as engineering, medicine, and agriculture.

A: When do you plan to send people to Mars?

B: The first manned mission is set to arrive on Mars in 2032.

A: How many colonists will you send at that time?

B: We are going to send four colonists on the first mission and four more every two years after that until there are twenty colonists living there.

A: How are they going to live?

B: Robots from the previous unmanned missions will prepare a living space for the colonists.

A: And how will the colonists get back home to Earth?

B: That's the most fascinating part of this journey. It's one way.

A

1. b 2. c 3. b
4. a

B

1. applicants 2. narrowed
3. manned 4. Mars
5. colonists

Going Up?

Reading p. 118

Comprehension Check

1. The idea has existed for more than one-hundred years.
2. It would need to be built near the Earth's equator.
3. It must be strong enough and light enough to withstand the Earth's gravitational pull.
4. Centrifugal force will hold it up and stop it from crashing into the earth.
5. Answers may vary.
   There would be no need to use rockets to deliver materials to space.
   It would be cheaper to send materials into space.
   It would be more convenient to send materials into space.

Wrap-up p. 120

A

1. smoke detector
2. memory foam
3. scratch-resistant lenses
4. water filter
5. solar panels
6. running machine

B

1. over
2. out
3. on
4. out
5. up
6. around

Unit 12 Accomplishments and Celebrations

He got it!

Vocabulary p. 122

1. a small controlled fire at a campsite or in a yard where people gather to stay warm, talk, or roast sausages or marshmallows
2. a ceremony commemorating the completion of high school, university, or a higher degree
3. a ceremony celebrating an annual remembrance
4. a gathering where people celebrate the career of a person who has decided to stop working
5. a Christian ritual involving the baptism of a child
6. a family get-together
7. a procession of decorated floats and performers that travel along a prearranged path
8. a gathering where people grill meat and enjoy a party together

Listening p. 123

Script

A: Hello. This is Mike speaking.

B: Mike, this is Katherine Spiegel.

A: Oh, hi, Katherine. I think your daughter and my son are friends.

B: Yes, that's right. Actually, I'm calling to invite your family to Stephanie's graduation party on June 2nd.

A: That's very nice of you. We'd be happy to attend. Oh, I just remembered that my nephew's graduation party is on the same day. What time is your party?

B: It starts at 7:00 p.m. We're just having an outdoor barbecue, so it's okay if you come after seven.

A: My nephew's party starts at 4:00 p.m., so that should give us plenty of time to get to your place by seven o'clock. Would you like us to bring anything?

B: No, not at all. We'll provide all of the food and beverages. Your family eats meat, right?

A: Yes, we do.

B: Good. We're having hamburgers, bratwurst, hot dogs, and, of course, cake.

A: Sounds wonderful. By the way, has Stephanie chosen a university yet?

B: Oh, yes. She was accepted to Penn State. She's pre-med.

A: Oh, congratulations! That's amazing. Steven is hoping to follow in Stephanie's shoes. He's only a sophomore right now, but he's working hard to get accepted to a good school like Penn.

A

1. c	2. c	3. b
4. a		

B

1. False	2. False	3. True
4. True		

You ran it in under three hours?

Listening p. 125

Script

1. My name is Yuki Tanaka, and I am 28 years old. I just finished my medical residency at a large hospital in Chicago, Illinois, in the United States. I worked really hard in school to get to this point. When all of my friends were going to parties in college, I spent all of my free time studying in the library. I have always dreamed of becoming a medical doctor one day, and now it has become a reality. My fiancé is also a medical doctor at the same hospital as me. We met during our residencies. He wants to be a surgeon, but I want to work in the emergency room. I like helping people, so I think the ER is the best place for me. It's a difficult job, and there are many nights that I don't get much sleep. But I love my job and my life. And I can't wait to get married in Jamaica next summer. I've never been there before!
2. Hey, I'm Sumin, and I just got my dream job. My boss called me into his office and said I would now be appearing on camera on the Live Shopping Network. I've been working as a production assistant at the Live Shopping Network for five years, but I never thought I'd have the opportunity to be on-screen talent. I told my roommate there was a zero-percent chance the Live Shopping Network would hire me as talent, but she disagreed. She recorded me while I pretended to sell items from our living room. I submitted the video to the producers, but I never thought in a million years they'd actually hire me. I'll be making a lot more money now, and I'll be working with some of my Live Shopping Network heroes. I have to pinch myself because this feels like a dream!

1. c	2. b	3. True
4. False	5. c	6. b
7. True	8. False	

My team worked hard on that project.

Grammar p. 126

B

1. made, stay
2. let, watch
3. get, to go
4. help, (to) pay
5. had, pulled
6. have, look

Listening p. 127

Script

A: Pearl, are you looking forward to graduating from university?

B: I have mixed emotions. On the one hand, it'll be nice to be done with classes. On the other hand, I need to find a job.

A: So you're not going to grad school?

B: I've thought about it, but I don't want to take out any more school loans. I need to start earning money.

A: Me, too. Do you have any job leads?

B: I'm a history major, so I don't even know what I can do with that. I'll probably end up in retail.

A: Ha-ha-ha! I'm a communications major. I'll probably end up in retail, too.

B: I'd really love to become a history professor. I love the ancient Roman period. How about you, Dillon?

A: I really want to become a screenwriter and film director. I'm actually thinking about moving to Los Angeles. Maybe I can get a job as a production assistant on a film or television show.

B: How exciting! Aren't you scared to move so far away from home?

A: A little, but it's my dream. If I go, I plan on taking some screenwriting classes in the evenings.

B: I loved your short stories in our creative writing class. They always made me laugh so hard.

A

1. b	2. a	3. b
4. a		

B

1. Pearl thinks she will work in retail after college.
2. Dillon and Pearl are graduating from college/university.
3. The ancient Roman period is Pearl's favorite period in history.
4. Pearl thinks Dillon's short stories were really funny.

The Wedding Planner

Reading p. 128

Comprehension Check

1. He was an assistant wedding planner for Gabrielle Barnett.
2. A wedding planner should be a great visionary and excellent coordinator.
3. He prefers to be direct, and he tells them the truth.
4. He advises couples to plan the wedding they want.

Wrap-up p. 130

A

1. bonfire
2. retirement party
3. anniversary party
4. parade
5. barbecues
6. graduation ceremony

B

1. helps, rake
2. makes, do
3. got, to teach
4. have, contact
5. had, painted
6. let, run